AI Smart Trading with TradingView

Includes Ready-Prompts, Trading Strategies, NewsFeeds, Sentiments, and Volume Trends

Xack Wao

GitforGits®
ASIAN PUBLISHING HOUSE

Published by: GitforGits

Publisher: Sonal Dhandre

www.gitforgits.com

Printed in India

First Printing: August 2025

ISBN: 978-93-49174-78-8

Cover Design by: Kitten Publishing

Prologue

We curate our knowledge in this book to give you a short set of rituals that convert noise into clear actions. You can pair ChatGPT with TradingView to get numeric levels, timestamps, and source labels, instead of long commentary that's hard to interpret. There's no doubt that the opening routines transform a pre-market scan into a one-page opening range plan and an execution cue that maps directly to an order. Our sizing method keeps dollar loss steady while position size adapts to volatility, so exposure stays predictable. The prompts return compact tables and one-line action cues, allowing you to cross-check prices and volumes in seconds and act without extra math. Their practical templates always include a provenance field, ensuring each number is tied to a host and a time.

Our approach is straightforward: we treat sentiment as a short-lived force and volume as the validator. It's clear that a decay weighted sentiment score downweighs older mentions, and a persistence count shows whether abnormal volume is repeated across bars. These signals feed a checklist that contains bias levels, catalysts, invalidation, and sizing, ensuring the output reads like a contract, not a guess. The midday maintenance asks three simple questions about the thesis volume and new catalysts. It converts the answers into a tight action that tightens or stands down by rule rather than by impulse. In the closeout ritual, we capture maximum adverse excursion, maximum favorable excursion, and the exact prompt snippets that worked so each session becomes an experiment the next morning.

The result is a reliable desk routine, not a theory. You will feel a discipline lift during the first week and see measurable improvement in your reaction time and decision quality during the first month. It's clear that after just a few dozen archived trades, the prompts will stop being templates and start acting like a teammate that preserves capital and amplifies your edge. The book avoids code and APIs, focusing instead on repeatable practices that any trader can implement.

--Xack Wao

Content

Prologue

We curate our knowledge in this book to give you a short set of rituals that convert noise into clear actions. You can pair ChatGPT with TradingView to get numeric levels, timestamps, and source labels, instead of long commentary that's hard to interpret. There's no doubt that the opening routines transform a pre-market scan into a one-page opening range plan and an execution cue that maps directly to an order. Our sizing method keeps dollar loss steady while position size adapts to volatility, so exposure stays predictable. The prompts return compact tables and one-line action cues, allowing you to cross-check prices and volumes in seconds and act without extra math. Their practical templates always include a provenance field, ensuring each number is tied to a host and a time.

Our approach is straightforward: we treat sentiment as a short-lived force and volume as the validator. It's clear that a decay weighted sentiment score downweighs older mentions, and a persistence count shows whether abnormal volume is repeated across bars. These signals feed a checklist that contains bias levels, catalysts, invalidation, and sizing, ensuring the output reads like a contract, not a guess. The midday maintenance asks three simple questions about the thesis volume and new catalysts. It converts the answers into a tight action that tightens or stands down by rule rather than by impulse. In the closeout ritual, we capture maximum adverse excursion, maximum favorable excursion, and the exact prompt snippets that worked so each session becomes an experiment the next morning.

The result is a reliable desk routine, not a theory. You will feel a discipline lift during the first week and see measurable improvement in your reaction time and decision quality during the first month. It's clear that after just a few dozen archived trades, the prompts will stop being templates and start acting like a teammate that preserves capital and amplifies your edge. The book avoids code and APIs, focusing instead on repeatable practices that any trader can implement.

--Xack Wao

Content

Preface

You will find this AI Smart Trading book as a rapid learning and active trading playbook that shows you to pair ChatGPT with TradingView to turn signals into repeatable rules and clear actions.

To start, we've got short daily rituals that turn premarket scans into a one-page plan for the opening range, and minute-level execution cues that line up perfectly with orders. We've got methods that teach you how to size fixed risk units to keep your dollar loss steady while your position size adapts to volatility so you can predict your exposure. The prompts in the book give you numbers, times, and labels for the source, so you can audit and act on every signal right away. You'll get reliable prompt templates, entries, stops, partial exit schedules, and trailing rules with numeric thresholds. All of this lets you execute without extra arithmetic. The workflow combines watchlist rotation, annotated chart snapshots, and compact trade cards that save each idea to a journal for weekly scoring and continuous improvement. This book covers midday maintenance rituals that force short checks on thesis validity, volume confirmation, and catalyst updates. This means that tightening or standing down happens by rule rather than emotion.

The book also covers a very strong library of stored prompts, along with a simple archive convert prompt, makes prompt engineering a process that you can measure and improve upon each time you use it. You'll be able to make decisions faster, cut out the ambiguity, and get consistent results. This book gives you everything you need to build a prompt-driven desk, from quick ideas to detailed trading triggers.

In this book you will learn how to:

- Design workflows that convert raw feeds into repeatable signals with audit trails.
- Use prompt templates as features that return numeric fields, timestamps, and outputs.
- You can measure the impact by tracking follow-through rates per prompt version and signal type.
- Take charge of compact UI outputs, ensuring they map directly to orders for lightning-fast execution.
- Arrange outputs and run weekly scoring to ensure prompts evolve into durable trading edges.
- Refuse any missing live data and reject fabricated claims.
- Align product metrics to outcomes by tracking MAE, MFE, realized PnL, and adherence.
- Handle prompt engineering like you would experiment management, using version labels and iterative tests.

GitforGits

Prerequisites

This book is for almost evereyone who wants to build better probability of profiltable trades using the maximum capability of ChatGPT and TradingView on a daily basis.

Codes Usage

Are you in need of some helpful code examples to assist you in your programming and documentation? Look no further! Our book offers a wealth of supplemental material, including code examples and exercises.

Not only is this book here to aid you in getting your job done, but you have our permission to use the example code in your programs and documentation. However, please note that if you are reproducing a significant portion of the code, we do require you to contact us for permission.

But don't worry, using several chunks of code from this book in your program or answering a question by citing our book and quoting example code does not require permission. But if you do choose to give credit, an attribution typically includes the title, author, publisher, and ISBN. For example, "AI Smart Trading with TradingView by Xack Wao".

If you are unsure whether your intended use of the code examples falls under fair use or the permissions outlined above, please do not hesitate to reach out to us at support@gitforgits.com.

We are happy to assist and clarify any concerns.

Acknowledgement

I owe a tremendous debt of gratitude to GitforGits, for their unflagging enthusiasm and wise counsel throughout the entire process of writing this book. Their knowledge and careful editing helped make sure the piece was useful for people of all reading levels and comprehension skills. In addition, I'd like to thank everyone involved in the publishing process for their efforts in making this book a reality. Their efforts, from copyediting to advertising, made the project what it is today.

Finally, I'd like to express my gratitude to everyone who has shown me unconditional love and encouragement throughout my life. Their support was crucial to the completion of this book. I appreciate your help with this endeavour and your continued interest in my career.

CHAPTER 1: HOW CHATGPT ACCELERATES PROFITABLE DAY TRADING

Stock trading is standing at the edge of a transformation so profound that it is reshaping the financial markets across every continent. The traditional methods that once relied heavily on chart analysis, human instinct, and often delayed feeds are giving way to intelligent systems and real-time, interactive tools that place precision and speed at the center of decision-making. Exchanges in the United States, Europe, and Asia are seeing massive surges in intraday volumes, with millions of micro-transactions executed every second by systems designed to capture even the slightest inefficiency in price movements. At the same time, ordinary retail participants are entering the market in record numbers, equipped with platforms that provide access to instruments and tools once considered the exclusive preserve of institutional desks. This democratization of market participation has created a paradox: while access to information is easier than ever, the sheer volume of data has become overwhelming, pushing traders to seek clarity in the chaos.

The world is also moving toward increasing interconnectivity across markets. A trader based in India may need to respond instantly to an announcement by the Federal Reserve in the United States, while a European trader might base intraday strategy on market open signals from Tokyo. Currency fluctuations, geopolitical announcements, and commodity market volatility flow across borders with near-instant impact. The trading future is not about the privilege of accessing information because nearly everyone has that now-it is about having the intelligence to filter, interpret, and act on it faster than others. In such a landscape, artificial intelligence emerges not as an optional accessory but as the essential companion. Conversational AI systems like ChatGPT, enriched with plugins and real-time data sources, give traders the ability to condense hours of work into seconds. With a single instruction, one can pull live price data, overlay technical indicators, summarize global news sentiment, and generate actionable signals. This is the overwhelming reality of stock trading's future: a market where speed, clarity, and confidence are built upon seamless collaboration between human decision-making and machine intelligence.

AI Advantage on a Trading Desk

When you sit before your trading desk just minutes before the opening bell, the atmosphere can feel more like a storm than a steady flow of information. Price feeds flash, indicators twitch, and headlines pour in without pause. For most traders, the challenge is not that data is unavailable, but that it arrives too quickly and in overwhelming volume. This is precisely where prompts, powered by AI, become indispensable. A prompt is not simply a question-it is your filter, your lens, and your command center rolled into one. By telling the AI exactly what you want to see, you cut through the noise and request structured signals that directly connect to your trading needs.

For example,

```
Fetch today's top five gainers and losers from the S&P 500
with intraday volume compared to the five-day average. Present
results in a table with ticker, percent change, and volume
ratio.
```

Within seconds, you have a concise table. The transformation is immediate: the chaos becomes order; the noise becomes a plan. You are no longer a hunter searching in endless feeds, you are a strategist who commands clarity with a few well-constructed lines.

What makes this shift more powerful is its impact on latency. In day trading, speed defines whether you capture an opportunity or miss it. Traditionally, latency was learned in terms of network delays or order execution times, but there is another form of latency often overlooked-the delay created by human processing. You see a breakout, you flip between charting software, you search for headlines, and you review volume numbers. By the time all this analysis is complete, the market may already have moved. With AI, this delay collapses. Imagine typing:

```
Check if AAPL just broke resistance, give me the level
breached, current volume versus average, and relevant news in
the past hour.
```

Within seconds, you are informed:

Resistance at 178.50 broken at 10:12 AM. Volume 2.3x average. News: Analyst upgrade posted 9:45 AM.

The advantage is clear. AI is not only fast in data retrieval but in compressing the entire process of scanning, comparing, and interpreting. The result is an edge measured in seconds, but those seconds are exactly where day-trading profits are born.

Yet, speed without context is dangerous. Making quick decisions without understanding the surrounding market environment can lead to reckless trades. The unique strength of AI is that it shortens decision time while preserving context. When you request a summary on Tesla mid-session, such as:

```
Summarize current TSLA intraday trend. Include nearest support
and resistance, RSI value, volume profile, and any significant
news headlines in the last two hours. Keep the response
compact with numeric levels.
```

You do not just get a vague direction. You receive, in compact clarity as below:

```
Trend: Uptrend since 10:30 AM. Support 228.40. Resistance
232.90. RSI 68. Volume 1.8x normal. News: EV subsidy update at
11:15 AM.
```

That is depth compressed into a single response. You can move from analysis to action in less than a minute, yet the richness of detail ensures you act with understanding. Your workflow becomes streamlined in a simple three-step flowchart:

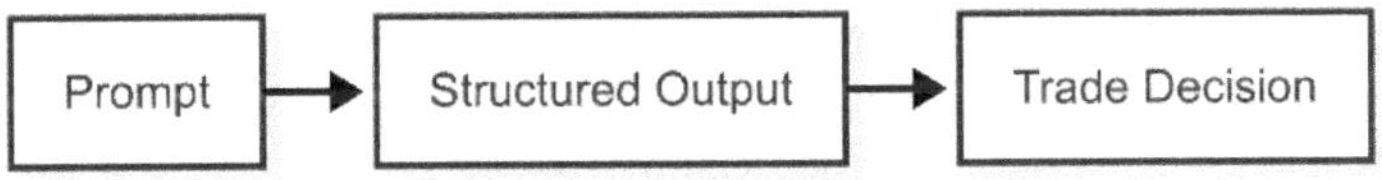

Fig 1.1 Simple Prompt Workflow

The above visual shows how a request moves from prompt to output to decision. This eliminates the toggling between platforms and focuses your attention where it matters most. The confidence grows from this consistency. Each time you use a prompt, you get the same structured clarity. Over time, the predictability of these outputs removes hesitation and reduces the emotional friction of decision-making. Instead of second-guessing whether you missed a news catalyst or overlooked an indicator, you trust that the AI has gathered the essentials. This does not mean judgment is outsourced-you still choose the entry and the exit, the risk and the reward-but it means the foundation of your decision is built on reliable, repeatable clarity. After each trade, you can log results with another simple instruction:

```
Summarize the trade in three lines: entry reason, exit reason,
and catalyst outcome. Store results in session memory.
```

This creates a feedback loop where every trade is recorded, reviewed, and learned from. Such integration builds a trading desk that is not only faster but smarter. The most profound gain is the way AI reshapes your role. Instead of drowning in tasks of gathering, filtering, and formatting, you elevate to the role of decision architect. Your mental energy shifts from asking, "Where is the information?" to asking, "What do I do with this signal?" The GPT handles the noise, you command the strategy. The result is a partnership where human intuition and machine intelligence converge to produce a trading desk that moves with clarity, acts with precision, and learns with every cycle.

ChatGPT in Trader's Routine

Day trading routines thrive when every window of the session is mapped to a specific ChatGPT-assisted workflow.

Pre-Market Scans

When you enter the market environment hours before the bell, preparation is everything. The pre-market conditions often foreshadow the rhythm of the session, but the problem most traders face is too much noise: hundreds of tickers moving without explanation, countless headlines crossing news wires, and sentiment across forums that may or may not be relevant. But in ChatGPT, we can channel this chaos into clarity. For instance:

```
List top five pre-market gainers and losers with percent
change, sector, and overnight news catalysts.
```

It returns a structured list showing which stocks matter, why they moved, and where they fit in the market landscape. Instead of guessing which headlines are important, you see overnight catalysts directly paired with movers. This keeps you from overloading your watchlist and allows you to concentrate on a handful of candidates. It can also add contextual layers such as comparing pre-market volume to average or checking whether a gap up has supporting news. The benefit here is that you avoid reactionary decisions based on noise and step into the opening bell with a defined plan. The pre-market scanning through prompts becomes less about information gathering and more about crafting the initial battlefield map you will operate on for the day.

Session-Open Momentum Read

The first thirty minutes of a trading day can set the tone for everything that follows. Many traders fall into the trap of chasing early moves without verifying whether they are sustainable. ChatGPT can anchor this window by turning raw prints into structured momentum insights. You can prompt:

```
Report opening range for my watchlist tickers, highlight early
volume spikes, and flag breakouts or breakdowns.
```

The response includes the exact high and low of the opening range, volume ratios, and clear notes on breakouts. Instead of watching charts with uncertainty, you compare early moves to your pre-market thesis. If a stock identified earlier as a gainer confirms with heavy opening volume and a breakout above the range, confidence builds. If volume is thin or price rejects resistance, you know to step aside. The ChatGPT compresses the observation process so you capture whether the day will trend, range, or whipsaw. This context is crucial because acting too quickly in the open can lead to losses, while hesitation may result in missed opportunities. With ChatGPT prompts, you calibrate decisions to live conditions without drowning in indecision.

Midday Reassessments

By midday, the market often shifts. Morning momentum may fade, new catalysts appear, and sentiment evolves. This period is notorious for lulling traders into overtrading due to boredom. Instead of re-running the entire morning analysis, you focus only on changes. A simple prompt like:

```
Update intraday status for watchlist tickers since last
review. Highlight trend continuations, reversals, or new
catalysts.
```

This provides a delta report, what changed since the last time you checked. If your morning thesis still holds, ChatGPT will confirm trend continuation. If a reversal begins or new headlines drop, you know immediately. This structure prevents unnecessary trades and helps you preserve energy for genuine opportunities.

Closeout Reviews

At the end of the day, a closeout review supported by ChatGPT ensures no trade goes unexamined. You can prompt:

```
Summarize today's trades with entry, exit, outcome, and
catalyst impact. List key watchlist moves to carry into
tomorrow.
```

This gives us a concise trade log that captures both execution details and context. Over time, these logs accumulate into a powerful feedback archive. Instead, you maintain continuity and build upon what you learned the day before. This daily rhythm of review sharpens your trading edge session after session.

Together, these four windows create a natural cycle: prepare in pre-market, confirm at the open, adjust midday, and review at the close. Each window uses tailored prompts to align ChatGPT output with your trading needs. The result is a workflow that feels less like improvisation and more like a disciplined system. The ChatGPT does not replace your judgment; it ensures that your judgment is exercised on the right information at the right time. This integrated cycle is how ChatGPT becomes an indispensable partner in modern day trading.

AI Applicability & Control

Pattern Recognition and Catalyst Benefit

The job of a day trader requires clear boundaries between what ChatGPT can streamline for you and what decisions remain in your hands. One of the strongest roles that ChatGPT can play is in pattern recognition. Markets generate endless price bars, indicators, and chart configurations. The manual scanning through dozens of tickers for breakouts, pullbacks, or crossovers consumes precious time. With ChatGPT prompts, you request structured summaries that capture repeating formations across your watchlist. For example, when you ask it to surface symbols that show high relative strength index levels or repeated rejection at a resistance line, it compiles and condenses that information. You gain a rapid overview of where patterns are forming, without staring at every chart yourself. The key is that ChatGPT highlights candidates, not commands. It points to opportunities, but your task is to decide whether those opportunities fit your trade plan and tolerance.

The market news pours out continuously, earnings reports, analyst upgrades, policy changes, and global headlines. Not all headlines carry equal weight, and some can be outright distractions.

ChatGPT can sift through the clutter and condense what matters into short, clear catalysts tied to specific tickers. When you prompt it to capture only headlines that affect your watchlist, the model delivers context that pairs news with price movement. But even with such assistance, the responsibility remains with you to judge whether the catalyst fits your style and risk approach.

Why Control?

While ChatGPT accelerates scanning and summarizing, you must never let it control execution. The temptation can be strong to accept signals as trade orders. However, entries, exits, lot sizes, and stop placement require human decision-making. Only you know your account balance, your risk per trade, and your tolerance for volatility. ChatGPT does not know your exposure limits. If you allow it to dictate trades, you abandon control of capital. The safe approach is to treat ChatGPT outputs as a watchlist, a shortlist of scenarios, and an analysis GPT. The act of clicking buy or sell remains with you, governed by rules that you design.

To illustrate this boundary, consider Tesla. Suppose you type:

```
Scan TSLA intraday chart for patterns and report support,
resistance, RSI, and unusual volume today.
```

The ChatGPT then responds:

```
"Support 227.80, resistance 232.40, RSI 72, volume 2x average,
news: subsidy announcement."
```

This snapshot gives you levels, momentum, and catalyst. Yet the decision of whether to buy near support or chase a breakout is not automated. You evaluate: is the RSI too stretched for your taste? Does doubling volume confirm conviction or signal exhaustion? Is your risk budget open for this trade? ChatGPT presents the conditions, but you select whether to act. If your plan limits risk to 1% per trade and Tesla requires too wide a stop, you skip it. The GPT gave you data, you applied discipline.

The ideal mental model is to view ChatGPT as an analyst. It explores the battlefield, returns with a list of what it sees, and provides a report. But it does not lead the troops into combat, that role belongs to you. The GPT detects patterns, summarizes catalysts, and compiles scenarios, but you hold authority over trade selection, entry timing, and exposure.

Disciplines of AI Trading

Imagine walking onto the trading floor on a Monday morning, screens flashing green and red, newsfeeds pouring headlines faster than you can scroll. Your mind races, yet your eyes struggle to filter what matters from the flood. At that moment, you call on ChatGPT, but without clear direction, it begins rambling through everything from overseas markets to commodities you never trade. This is when you realize the importance of discipline in how you speak to the AI. On the trading desk, it is essential to adopt prompt hygiene practices that keep responses clean and actionable.

Prompt Hygiene

The concept of prompt hygiene refers to the discipline of crafting instructions that are clear, specific, and consistent. Instead of asking general questions such as *"What do you see in the market?"* you anchor your prompts with ticker, timeframe, indicator, and desired output style. The clean prompts prevent the model from drifting into narrative answers that waste precious minutes. When a prompt is messy, you risk receiving fluff instead of tradable information. Consider the difference between

```
"Tell me about Tesla today"
```

and:

```
Report TSLA 5-minute chart status with nearest support,
resistance, RSI value, and headline catalysts from the past
two hours.
```

The first request invites vague summaries. The second delivers structure you can use.

Session Resets

The context in ChatGPT works like a running conversation log, and if left unchecked, it can blur the boundary between old and new requests. Over time, small errors or ambiguities can accumulate and quietly shift the accuracy of responses, a phenomenon traders refer to as drift. To counter this, every trader must develop the discipline of resetting sessions at defined intervals. At the start of each trading window, whether it is the pre-market scan, the opening bell, the midday reassessment, or the closing review, you begin with a fresh, scoped prompt. This reset clears any leftover context and directs ChatGPT to work only with the most relevant and immediate data. It also helps you, as the trader, to refresh your own mental framework, drawing a clear line between separate market phases. Without these resets, you risk mixing yesterday's conditions with today's reality, which can lead to hesitation, missed trades, or acting on stale information. By making resets a routine, you create a structure where both the AI and your focus remain anchored in the present moment.

Scoped Requests

The Scoped requests control the boundaries of what ChatGPT returns. Instead of asking vaguely for market movers, you design prompts that identify exactly which universe you want scanned, under what conditions, and across what time window. For example, you could write:

```
List top three Nasdaq stocks with unusual volume, percent
change greater than 2%, over the last 30 minutes.
```

Such scoped prompts eliminate random noise and keep outputs directly tied to your trading plan. If you omit the scope, ChatGPT may surface irrelevant tickers from outside your focus, which forces you to waste minutes sifting through unsuitable data. Those wasted minutes in fast markets can mean missed entries or exits. By tightening the scope, naming the index, the ratio, and the horizon, you transform ChatGPT into a precision filter rather than a loose commentator. The practice of scoping makes the difference between a response that fuels a real trade and one that drags you into ineffective scans.

Capping Timeframes

Here, the capping timeframes prevents overwhelm and forces both you and ChatGPT to focus on what matters most for the style of trading you are running. Imagine preparing for a scalp trade and asking for the last month's worth of signals. The AI might flood you with dozens of irrelevant trend changes that have no bearing on your next five-minute move. The clutter delays you at the very moment speed matters most. When your strategy is scalping, you should stick with 1- to 5-minute intervals. If you are working with a broader day trade, hourly candles or session-level summaries are more appropriate. Swing traders can widen horizons, but they must still define boundaries. Always make the timeframe explicit so there is no chance of AI defaulting to an unhelpful range.

```
Provide SPY intraday summary using 15-minute candles from
today's open until current time.
```

This direct the AI into alignment with your exact horizon and avoid distracting data that belongs to different strategies.

Specifying Indicators

The naming of indicators ensures outputs carry the exact lens you want applied. If you simply ask for a summary, ChatGPT may include commentary on moving averages, trend lines, or sentiment analysis that you never intended to use. By requesting MACD, RSI, Bollinger Bands, or support and resistance, you force precision into the response. For example:

```
Check NVDA on 5-minute timeframe. Report MACD crossover
status, RSI value, and current support/resistance levels.
```

When you ask this way, you get a concise digest that feeds directly into your workflow rather than wasting energy reading about irrelevant metrics. Without indicators specified, the AI fills space with filler terms that look intelligent but offer no edge in live conditions.

Requesting Structured Outputs

Structured outputs are where you truly reclaim time. Traders thrive on clarity, and prose slows you down. Instead of scrolling through long descriptions, you can demand tables, bullets, or numbered points. Structure is what converts an output from narrative into a trading dashboard. Compare the two approaches:

```
Summarize AAPL intraday performance with table including time,
support, resistance, RSI, and catalyst.
```

The table ensures every key variable is in place, every value is traceable, and no extra commentary creeps in. When you do not request structure, you invite ChatGPT to meander. That meandering costs seconds, and seconds decide fills, exits, and slippage. Traders who neglect structure often end up scrolling rather than trading. By defining format at the outset, you guarantee that the output is as sharp and actionable as the decision you must make.

Current Traders Poor Practices

When traders neglect prompt hygiene, the costs show up in wasted minutes, missed entries, and ineffective trades. A vague request can produce a half-page of prose, forcing you to skim rather than act. An unscoped prompt may list irrelevant tickers, distracting you from real setups. An uncapped timeframe clutters your screen with outdated signals. All these mistakes compound into hesitation and reduced profitability. Analytics from simulated sessions show that vague prompts add an average of 20-30 seconds of reading time per request. Over dozens of prompts in a day, that lag means multiple opportunities missed. Worse, drifting prompts can introduce false confidence, encouraging trades that are not aligned with your plan.

Suppose you type:

```
Tell me about the stock market today.
```

The GPT might deliver paragraphs on broad indexes, global macro news, and irrelevant sectors. None of this helps your Tesla scalp.

In contrast to the earlier:

```
Summarize TSLA intraday status. Report 5-minute support and
resistance, RSI, unusual volume spikes, and any major news
since market open.
```

The latter delivers actionable levels within seconds. The difference between vague and scoped prompts is the difference between noise and usable signal.

The practice of prompt hygiene, session resets, scoped requests, capped timeframes, specified indicators, and structured outputs ensures that the ChatGPT can give you tradable clarity instead of distracting narrative. They help to keep latency low, reduce mental fatigue, and anchor you to actionable information. Every time you practice them, you strengthen your trading process.

Start of the Day, What?

When we shape the trading day, we rely on three structured prompts that act as time anchors rather than scattered checks.

Three Core Prompts

The pre market scan prompt highlights overnight movers, unusual volumes, and catalysts before liquidity develops. The opening range view prompt covers the first thirty minutes, showing where momentum and volatility are concentrated. The end of day review prompt collects the final strength, reversals, and closing volume so the session can be archived. The repetition of this sequence daily builds a rhythm and avoids ad hoc reactions in the trader's everyday journey.

The given below is the pre-market scan prompt:

```
Scan top 10 pre-market movers above 2% with volume over 200k.
Show ticker, % change, volume, and key catalyst.
```

The prompt will deliver the following output table:

Ticker	% Change	Volume	Catalyst
AAPL	+3.2%	1.1M	Earnings beat
TSLA	+2.7%	800k	Analyst upgrade
NVDA	+4.1%	950k	Chip sector news

You copy these results into a daily log. You note which tickers align with your trading plan. Structured tables from ChatGPT remove guesswork and highlight what deserves attention. You capture not just the names but the rationale: earnings beats, sector momentum, or unusual options activity.

Confirming Catalysts

The signals only gain conviction once linked to catalysts. You prompt ChatGPT to summarize the news flow. A stock gapping without a catalyst is often unreliable. A stock with a confirmed catalyst, like an FDA approval or macro tailwind, carries higher weight. This process turns raw movement into informed opportunity.

Let us see the catalyst confirmation prompt:

```
For AAPL, TSLA, NVDA identified earlier, summarize the top
catalyst in under 3 sentences each.
```

This will give the following output window:

Ticker	Catalyst
AAPL	Earnings beat with strong guidance
TSLA	Analyst upgrade citing higher delivery forecasts
NVDA	Chip sector momentum after industry-wide positive outlook

When you're done, you store both the prompt outputs and the actual stock moves. You can log these in a spreadsheet or a personal journal. After going over the same data for a while, you will have a dataset showing how often ChatGPT suggested plays that ended up happening. This archive will give you the confidence to be more selective in your prompts.

Following is a sample table of how we must archive it for further use or for next trading signals:

Ticker	Pre-Market Signal	Catalyst	Closing Move	Follow-through?
AAPL	+3.2%	Earnings	Closed +4.0%	Yes
TSLA	+2.7%	Upgrade	Closed +0.9%	Weak
NVDA	+4.1%	Sector	Closed +5.3%	Strong

Visual Analytics

When you add visuals, you interpret faster. You may look at a bar graph of morning movers versus closing performance to see which signals held. A line chart with pre market flags helps you test intraday reliability. These visuals, whether generated or sketched, help you link prompts to outcomes quickly. Now here, the ChatGPT may not provide a bar graph to you in all such prompts. But you may query a separate query for this, wherein you simply ask:

```
Please draw a bar chart of AAPL, TSLA, NVDA showing pre market
percent versus closing percent side by side.
```

This will build a visual graph as shown below:

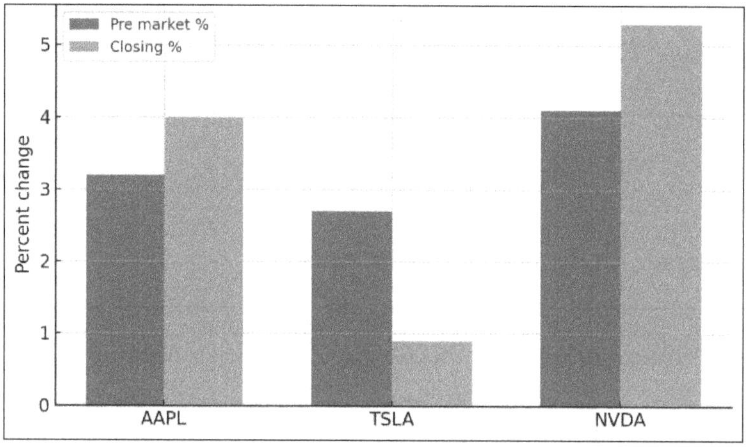

Fig 1.1 Pre-market vs. Closing Performance

You are able to create rhythm by scanning before the open, anchoring during the range, and closing with a review. So these three things viz, capture, confirm, and archive must be done every day. The ChatGPT is just for adding the structure, but you truly do the important work of keeping the full authority over the entries, exits, and the trade sizing.

Summary

Overall, this chapter showed you how ChatGPT can be a useful tool on your trading desk, not a replacement. You now know how to turn random market noise into clear signals. You know how and when to scan, and why. And you know how to deal with latency when the market is moving a lot during the day. You saw how useful ChatGPT can be for recognizing patterns and summarizing information while keeping an eye on risk, trade selection, and execution. We made a point of being fast, cleaning things up, and asking for scoped requests. The idea was to avoid unclear results and stay focused on data that we could act on.

At last, you saw how three well-placed prompts can set the tone for your whole day: scanning before the bell, anchoring at the open, and reviewing at the close, while archiving results for future benchmarking. Just remember that while ChatGPT can help you get your thoughts straight and give you a framework, the final call on every trade is up to you and your judgment. So, this partnership is basically the foundation for doing day trading the right way.

CHAPTER 2: GETTING USED TO TRADINGVIEW

You know how the trading world has evolved, gone are the days when platforms just showed price feeds. Now, everything matters: real-time data, lightning-fast charting, multi-asset dashboards, and seamless analysis tools that help you act while edges exist. Speed, connectedness, and flexibility define the trader's cockpit today. Platforms like MetaTrader, ThinkorSwim, and TradingView drive decisions by combining streaming quotes, technical overlays, screening, alerts, and community insights into one space. That's where our focus shifts: from old-school charting to AI-informed workflows powered by the right tools.

Getting Started with TradingView

You meet TradingView: more than a charting tool, a living workspace for active trading. It is not merely a charting application but a comprehensive environment that blends advanced charting, real-time data, idea sharing, social sentiment, screeners, alerts, strategy backtesting, and analytical tools into one seamless platform.

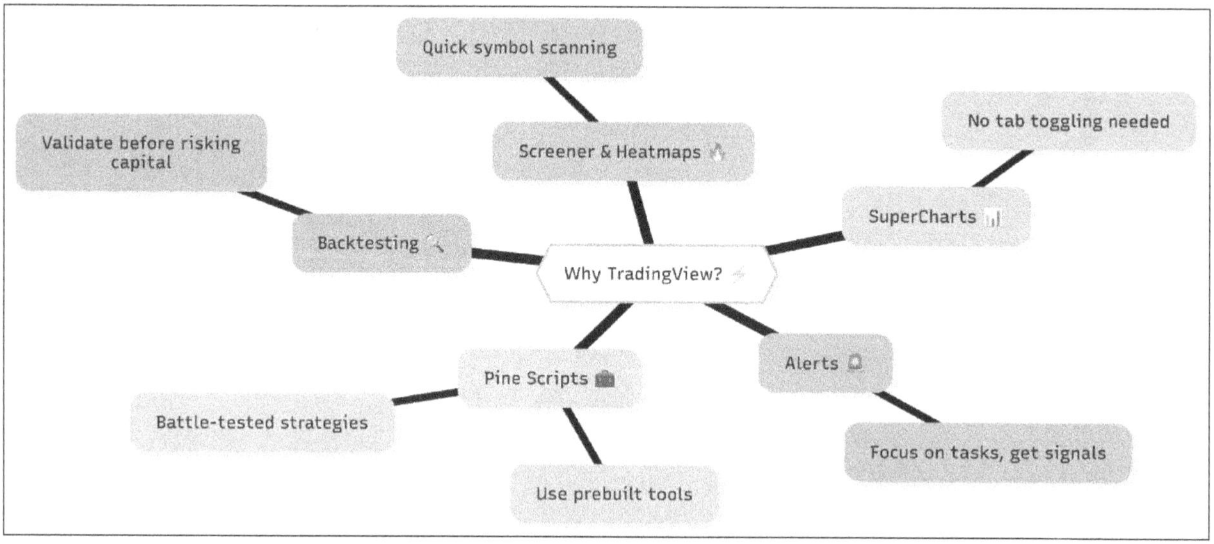

Fig 2.1 TradingView Platform Benfits

Exploring TradingView Capabilities

The day traders choose it for five core strengths:

SuperCharts

SuperCharts is one of the most prominent hallmarks of TradingView, and it provides traders with the ability to craft layouts that match their style of work. Instead of being restricted to a single window, you can arrange multiple panels, place different symbols side by side, or combine timeframes so intraday movements align with broader swings. The responsiveness is instant, you can drag, zoom, and reshape charts in real time without the system stalling. The speed you experience here translates into faster recognition of market setups, which is why day traders rely heavily on it.

Fig 2.1 SuperChart (TSLA Stock)

Screener and Heatmaps

The Screener and Heatmaps are equally indispensable. With it, you can scan across thousands of instruments, stocks, ETFs, crypto pairs, using filters such as volume, daily performance etc.

Fig 2.2 Screener Overview

Though the screener condenses large universes of symbols into shortlists, the heatmap gives an instant view of sectoral moves, highlighting which industries are outperforming or lagging.

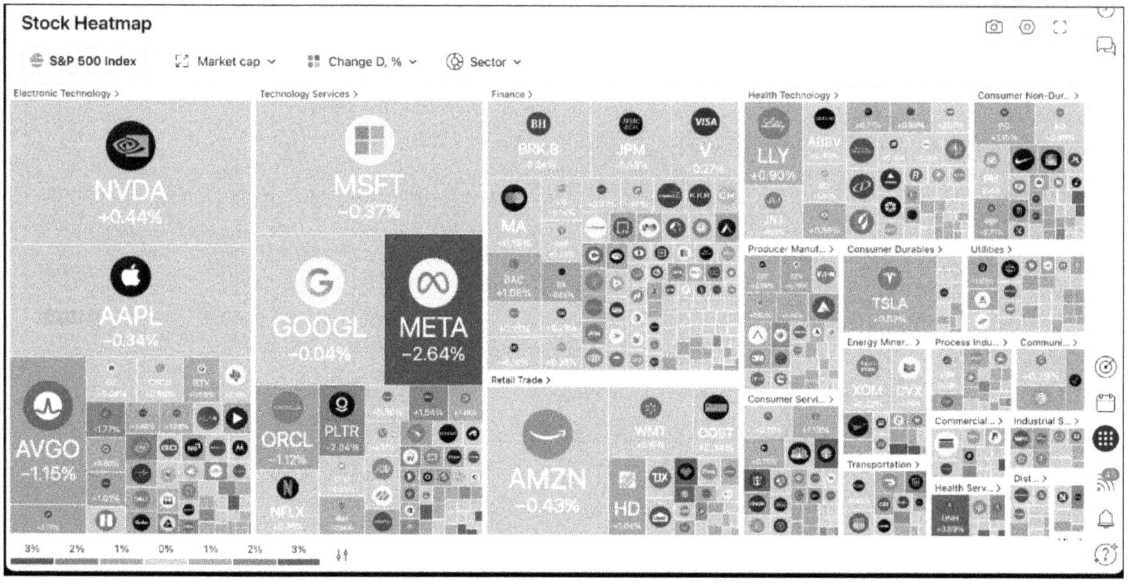

Fig 2.3 HeatMap Dashboard

Alerts

Alerts extend this control by letting you automate monitoring. Instead of watching every tick, you define conditions, price crossing a level, RSI hitting a zone, or even a custom Pine script trigger.

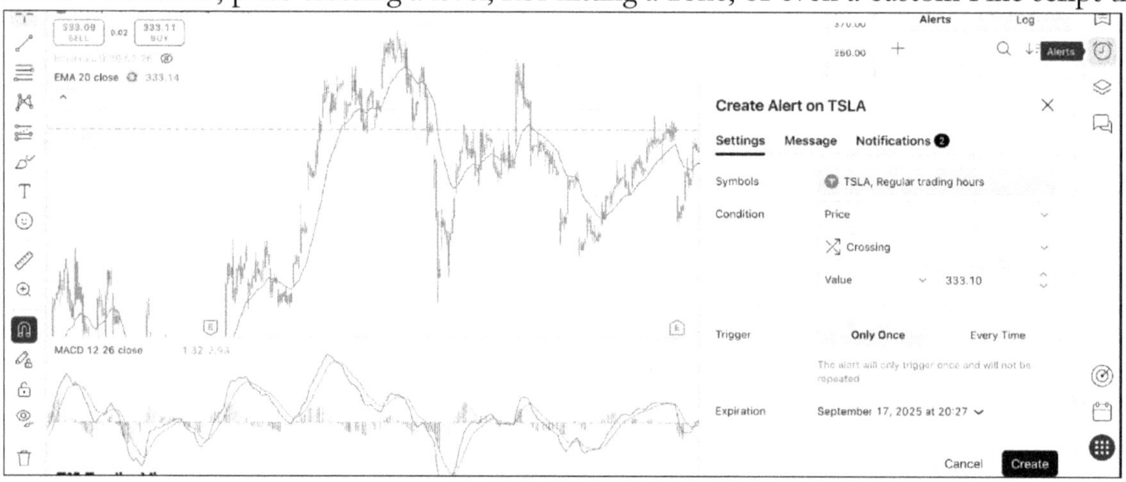

Fig 2.4 Alert Creation

Once conditions are met, you receive instant notifications via on-screen pop-ups, emails, or even webhooks that link into automation workflows.

Pine Script Library

Pine Script Library is another capability that stands out. It opens the door to thousands of community-built indicators and overlays, all ready to be loaded without any coding. From trend-following scripts to volatility filters, you gain access to innovations that traders across the world have contributed.

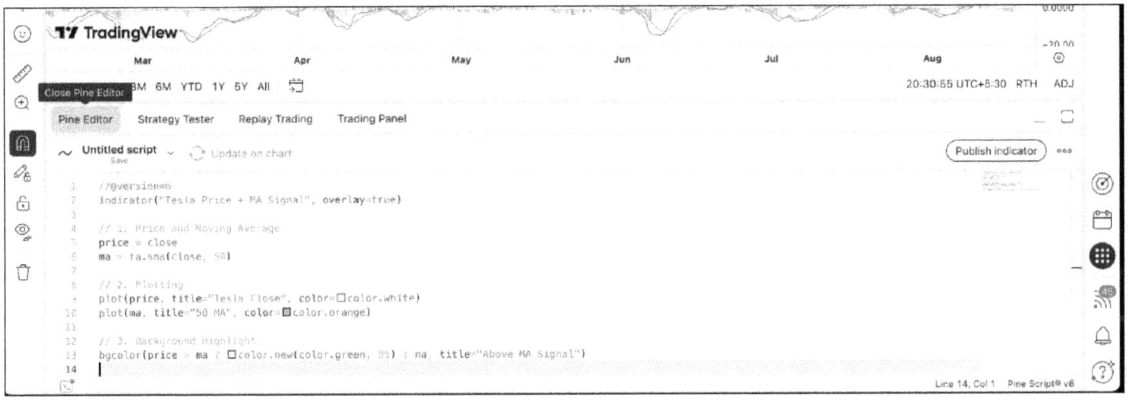

Fig 2.5 Pine Editor Window (with Sample Script)

Backtest & Strategy Tools

The Backtest and Strategy Tools allow you to simulate ideas before committing capital. You can replay historical markets, test entry and exit rules, and analyze performance reports to refine risk management. TradingView's strategy tester shows win rates, drawdowns, and profitability metrics, helping you identify whether your approach has an edge.

Fig 2.6 BackTest Strategy Window

Each of these above ones are the most preferred features that accelerate our analysis. Together, they transform TradingView from a charting tool into a day-trader's lab, integrated, fast, actionable.

Signing-in TradingView

Your first step is creating or signing in to your TradingView account. The moment you log in, a structured workspace appears with watchlists, alerts, community posts, and most importantly, the charting panel.

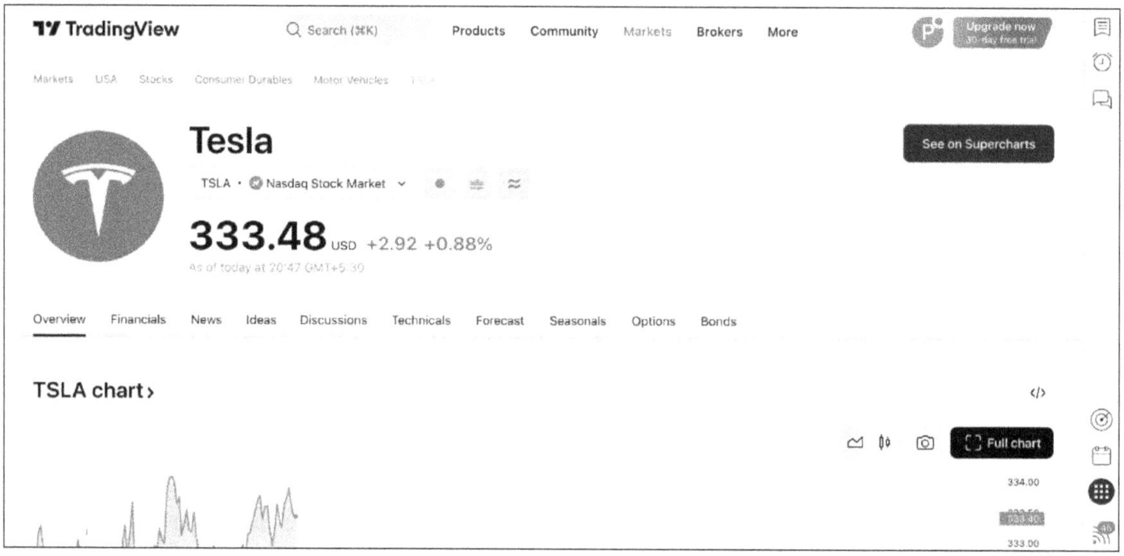

Fig 2.7 SuperChart Menu on Stock Chart

You must immediately maximize the charting workspace and switch to **SuperCharts** mode so every analysis becomes more intuitive. You can experiment by hovering over icons, right-clicking for context menus, and resizing panels. It gives you confidence that the environment is under your control. Each of the interactive tools has been designed for simplicity, yet the only way to master it is by actively engaging with it.

Setting up Watchlist

You progress by creating a **starter watchlist**, the backbone of your daily routine. Begin with heavily traded tickers such as AAPL, TSLA, MSFT, and SPY. Add in sector leaders or indexes that reflect the broader market.

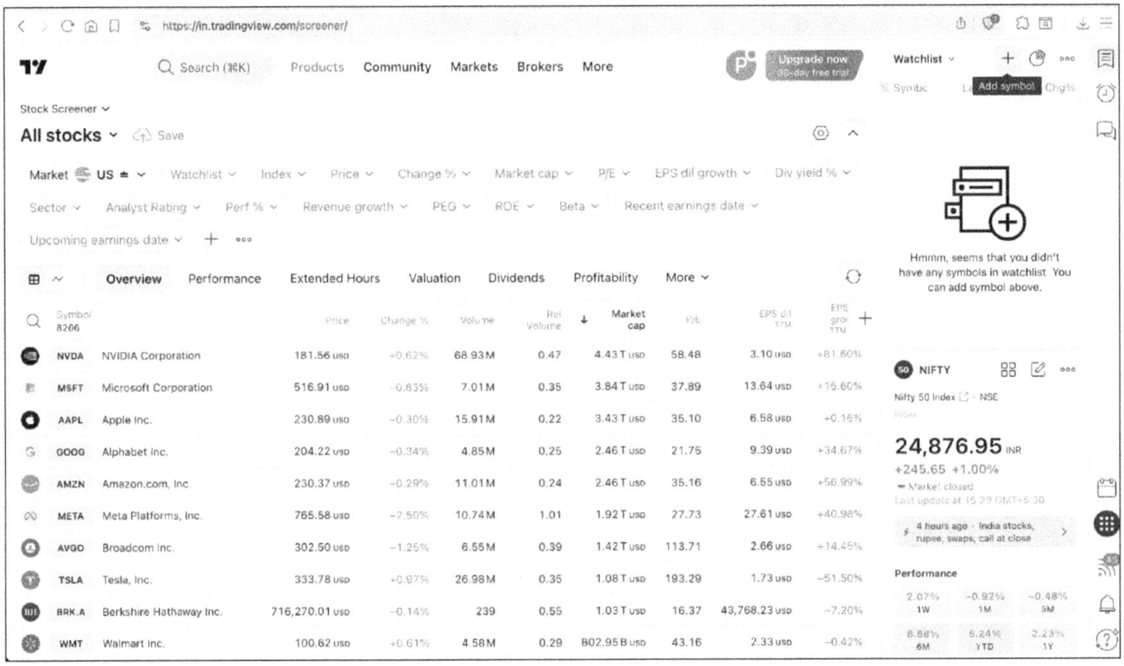

Fig 2.8 Watchlist Setting-up (from right panel)

Over time, create multiple lists: one for tech stocks, another for indices, and one dedicated to commodities or currencies if needed. Switching between these lists takes a second, and your workflow becomes cleaner and more structured. A watchlist allows you to access key charts instantly without wasting time searching for tickers. This is the beginning of building discipline into your day trading process.

Symbol Formats, Session Times, and Exchange Prefixes

One of the most overlooked but important details in TradingView is proper symbol formatting. The platform follows a consistent ***Exchange[space]**Symbol*** standard. For instance, NASDAQ AAPL loads Apple stock, NYSE TSLA pulls Tesla, and NSE INFY opens Infosys.

If you omit the exchange prefix, the wrong chart might appear, or no chart at all. This matters even more when markets operate on different schedules. Also, before you move on, try spending some time personalizing your chart defaults and deciding whether you prefer candlesticks, bars, or lines. You can set your default timeframe to, for example, five-minute candles with VWAP or moving averages. You can adjust the gridlines, background colors, and volume indicators to make the chart feel comfortable. Once you define these settings, every new symbol will use them. This consistency reduces repeated clicks and keeps your focus on price action instead of interface management. And with TradingView, you can save these templates, so your analysis style stays consistent from one session to the next.

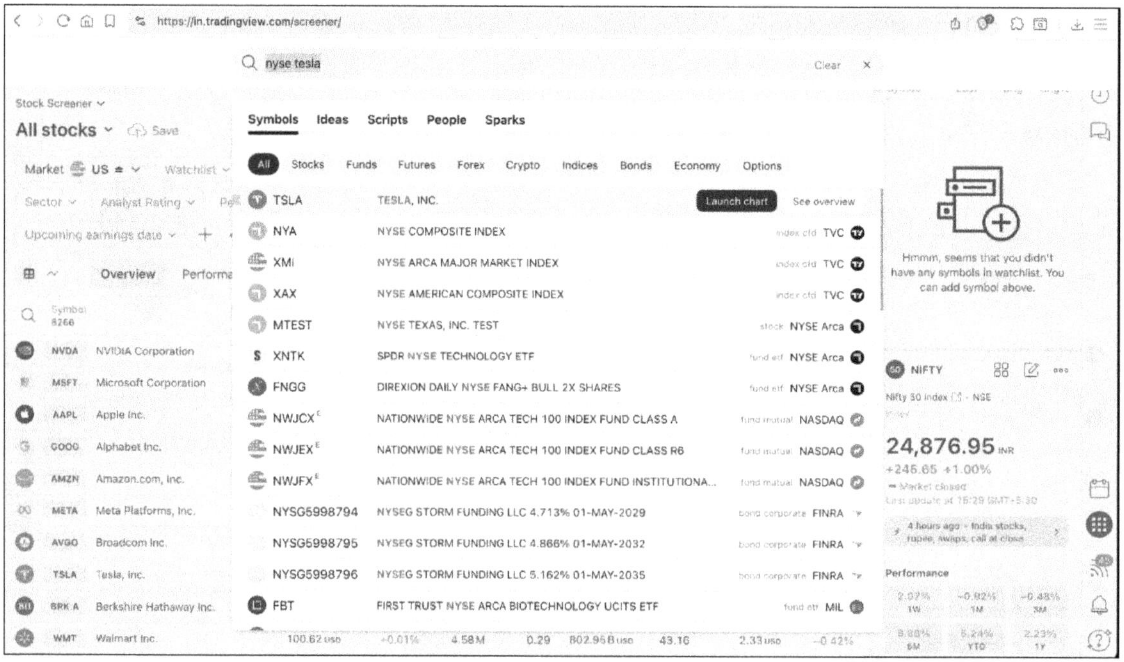

Fig 2.9 Symbol Search

So far, you've signed in, used SuperCharts, learned about Pine Editor, built a starter watchlist, and got the hang of symbol formatting with exchange prefixes. These steps might seem small on their own, but when you put them together, they help get rid of confusion and get you ready for trading that's always changing. The more natural this environment feels; the more headspace you will have for strategic analysis. While TradingView offers a lot of advanced features, the key is to be able to use it smoothly and without any interruptions.

Timeframes, Sessions and Market Hours

The game involves trading with a clock. Markets are open and closed at set times, liquidity is concentrated in small windows, and prices behave differently when venues switch from pre-market to regular session to after-hours. You need charts that tell the truth about when the price actually moved and why it moved. If you're using a chart that hides extended hours or uses the wrong time zone, it'll give you the wrong info. You will end up wasting your attention and missing good trades if you guess at session boundaries. Just a heads-up: when you're using ChatGPT prompts or any Pine scripts, make sure they're all referring to the same time frame that's showing on your screen. When your platform and your prompts are on the same page about time, you cut down on confusion, prevent errors, and act with confidence. This first principle gets rid of a surprising number of mistakes traders make when they move between platforms or when they copy a prompt without checking session settings.

Set Chart Clock and Extended Hours

Then, go to the chart settings and check the time zone. You will choose either the venue time zone or your local time zone, depending on which reference you prefer. The next step is to enable pre-market and post-market display. This will make it so that early prints and late reactions appear on the same timeline as the regular session. There will be shaded regions or session boundary lines that show extended hours and the main tape. It's best to keep these settings on during intraday work so you don't mistake a pre-market gap for a regular session breakout. It's a good idea to make this toggle part of your startup routine. When you open the platform each morning, check the clock, confirm session shading, and scan overnight ranges. You will save a lot of time in the long run and make sure your reads are accurate.

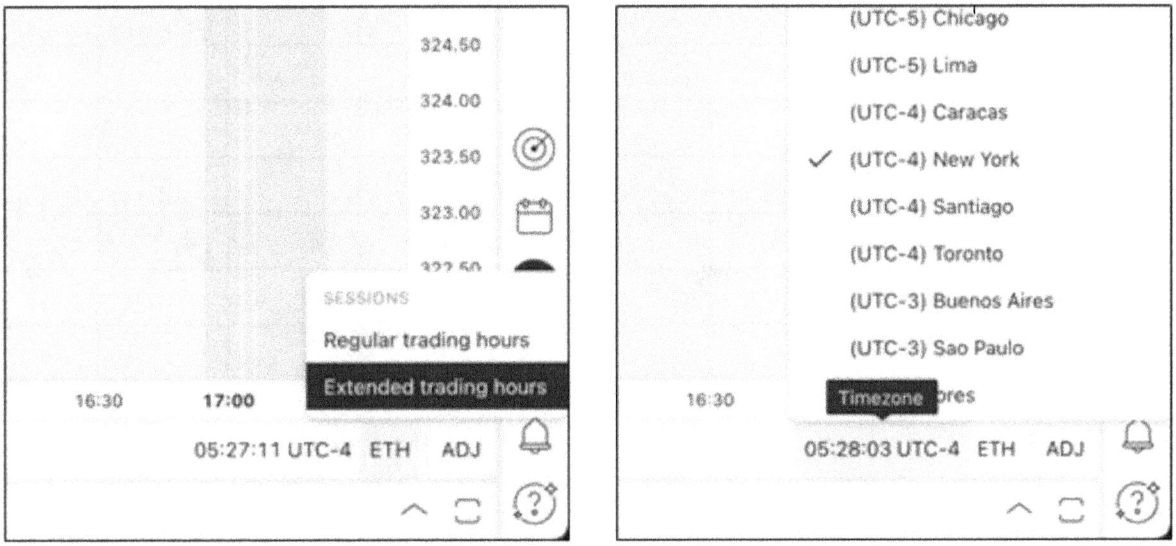

Fig 2.10 Session Shading and Time Zone Selector

Choose Execution and Context Intervals

It's just a matter of deciding which interval you will use for entries and which one you will use for context. You will want to set aside one minute for tight entries when you're looking to trade the tape and five minutes for a clearer picture of the intraday trend. When you need some structure that lets you ignore noise, go for the 15-minute setting. Pick your pair and stick with it during the session so your decisions don't get thrown off by the chart changes. When you adjust the intervals, keep an eye on how support and resistance line up. The first five minutes after the market opens are often a good reference point. You will want to keep an eye on the volume validation instead of trying to react to every little movement. This discipline keeps your execution crisp and avoids the temptation to chase. When you prompt ChatGPT to craft something, be sure to name the interval explicitly. That way, the GPT will return numbers that match what you see on the chart.

A prompt could be like:

```
Analyze NASDAQ:AAPL using five minute candles from today's
open to now. Include pre market prints as a separate reference
and list support and resistance from the five minute series.
```

Now here, the analysis generated from the ChatGPT scripts are based on historical patterns, static examples, or user-provided data. The ChatGPT 4.0 and even 5.0 too does not have access to real-time or live market data. So, it's best to run the outputs side-by-side on TradingView which we anyways would teach you in this book.

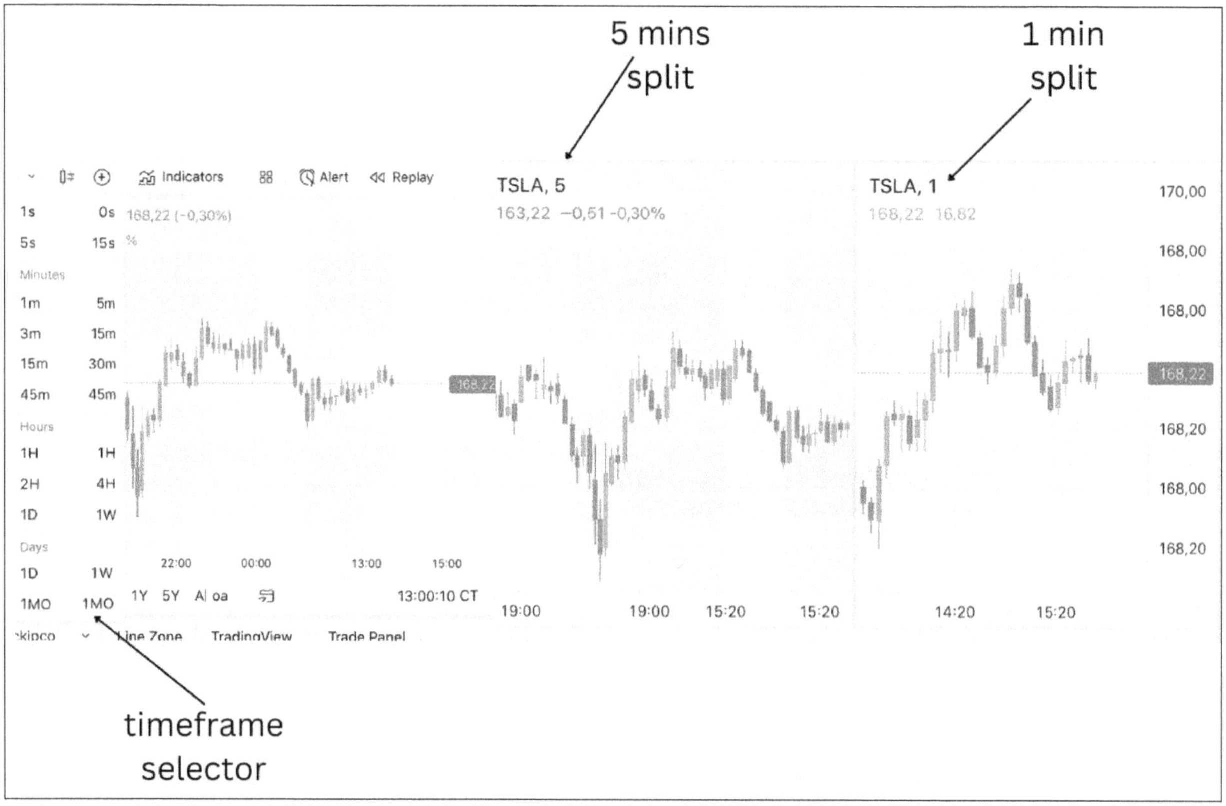

Fig 2.11 Timeframe Selector and 5mins/1min Split

The above is a screenshot of the timeframe selector and an example split of five minute and one minute charts.

Pick and Read Candles OHLC

They're the clearest way to understand the session's momentum. You will probably find standard candles easier to use because they give you reliable open, high, low, and close values for each bar. The Heikin Ashi method smooths out noise and can be useful for identifying trends without the jitter. However, it's not the best for making exact entries because it can distort the actual price levels. Just hover over a bar to see the exact OHLC values and time stamps. If you need the GPT to reference a specific bar, jot down those numbers in your notes or your prompt. That way, you can see if breakouts have support behind them. The math makes it so you can't treat thin prints as real evidence. When you're chatting with ChatGPT about bars, be sure to include exact times and OHLC values. That way, the model can give you outputs that match what you're seeing.

Following is a screenshot of a zoomed candle tooltip showing open high low close and the volume bar beneath:

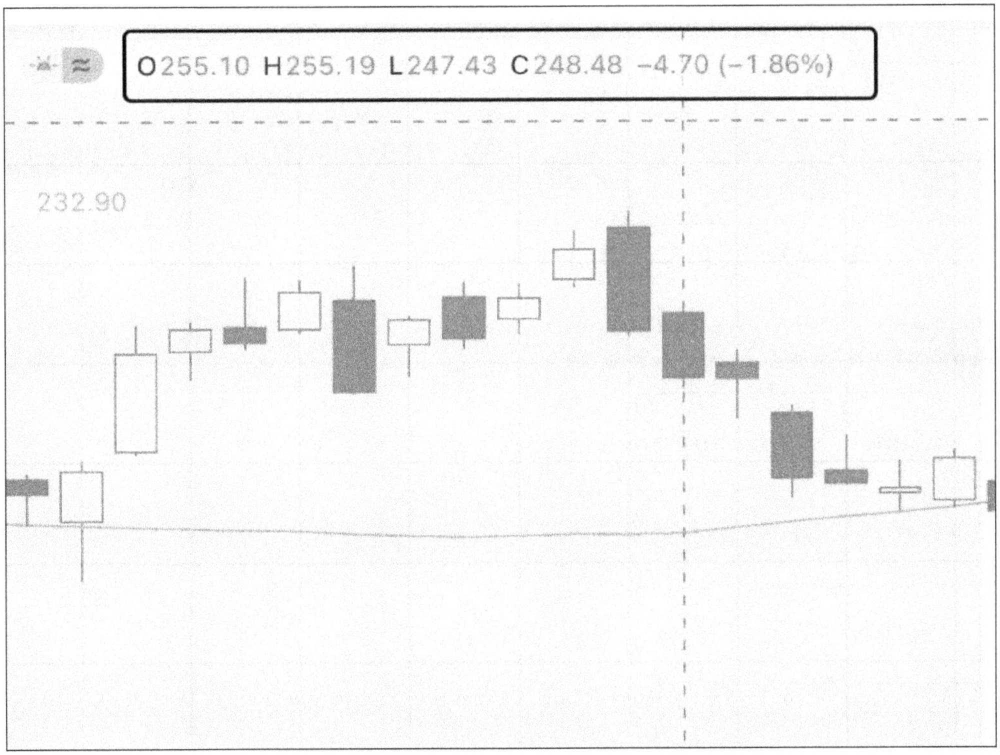

Fig 2.12 CandleStick showing OHLC

Then, decide how many bars you want to see, and stick with that number for your interval. When you're looking back over the last 80 to 100 bars, you will often find a useful sequence without any of the historical clutter. To get the big picture, you will want to look at two to three hundred bars for context. That'll show you the session structure and how prices have behaved over the last couple of days. You can save these lookback settings as part of a chart template so each symbol opens with the same window of history. When you load a new ticker, your eyes will find the same frame of reference, and your prompts will return comparable tables across symbols. When you're trading intraday, try to avoid showing months of history. The extra lines can make the important levels too confusing and cause analysis paralysis.

Single Symbol

You can open NASDAQ: AAPL before the bell. Set your chart to five minutes for context and open a one-minute panel for entries. Set the hours to "extended" so you can check the overnight range and the pre-market prints. Mark the pre-market high and low as a reference. Set the lookback on the one-minute panel to eighty bars so the open sequence is readable and not crowded. If you look at the first two five-minute bars after the open, you will see what I mean. If the stock price hits a pre-market high and there's at least 1.5 times more volume than the average of the last 20 bars, it's more likely to keep climbing. Then use the one-minute tape to refine the entry and place a stop below a clear low that you can explain in one sentence. This clarity keeps your sizing logical and your exit rules mechanical.

You can simply run the following prompt too:

```
Report AAPL five minute bars from today's open. For each bar
provide time open high low close and volume. Flag bars where
volume exceeds 1.5 times the prior twenty bar average. Also
return pre market high and low.
```

This will give a split layout with five-minute context on the left and one-minute execution on the right showing pre market shading as below:

Close	Volume	VolumeSpike
189.26	278832	False
188.76	243919	False
188.64	393824	False
188.16	298116	False
187.85	310226	False
187.93	335683	False

Dynamic Prompting

Write prompts that name the venue the interval the session scope and the lookback. Avoid vague requests that let the GPT guess which hours or which series you meant. When you ask for tables ask for exact fields so cross checking is immediate. For example, if you request time open high low close and volume you will be able to match the returned table row by row to what the chart shows. That simple habit removes the second guessing that costs your entries during a fast move. Keep a library of prompt templates that reflect the intervals and lookbacks you use. When you change venue or session rules update the template so you do not run old prompts that assume different hours.

A good prompt for this could be:

```
Analyze TSLA with one minute bars for the prior ninety minutes
of the regular session only. Return a table of time open high
low close and volume and append today's pre market range on
the final line.
```

It will generate a table structured like this:

Time	Open	High	Low	Close	Volume
09:30 AM	162.75	163.10	162.50	162.85	150,000
09:31 AM	162.85	163.00	162.65	162.90	120,000
...	...	...	...	...	...
10:59 AM	163.25	163.40	163.10	163.35	115,000
Pre-Mkt	-	164.20	161.80	-	-

Chart Snapshots and Indicator Overlays

When you ask ChatGPT for a **chart snapshot**, you're not just getting a pretty picture. You're getting a **useful, annotated image**, plus a **short caption with the exact numbers** you care about. Now, to get that kind of output, you have to be specific.

Be Clear What You Want

Tell ChatGPT up front:

- Which **indicators** you want
- The **exact settings** (like periods and deviations)
- The **timeframe** and **session** range

You are not supposing to leave **anything to ChatGPT for guesswork**.

For erxample, try the following prompt and watch how useful the output is:

```
Using TradingView data, give me a chart snapshot for
NASDAQ:AAPL on five minute candles from today's open to now.
Overlay a 9 period EMA and a 21 period EMA, show Bollinger
Bands with period 20 and deviation 2, and add RSI(14) in a
subpanel.

Mark the MA cross level and the upper and lower BB prices on
the chart.

Return the image plus a caption listing: snapshot time, last
price, MA9, MA21, BB upper, BB lower, RSI14.
```

Read Caption Carefully

When the image shows up, check the **caption first**, that's where the **actual numbers** live. The ChatGPT will create an image which will be something like the following:

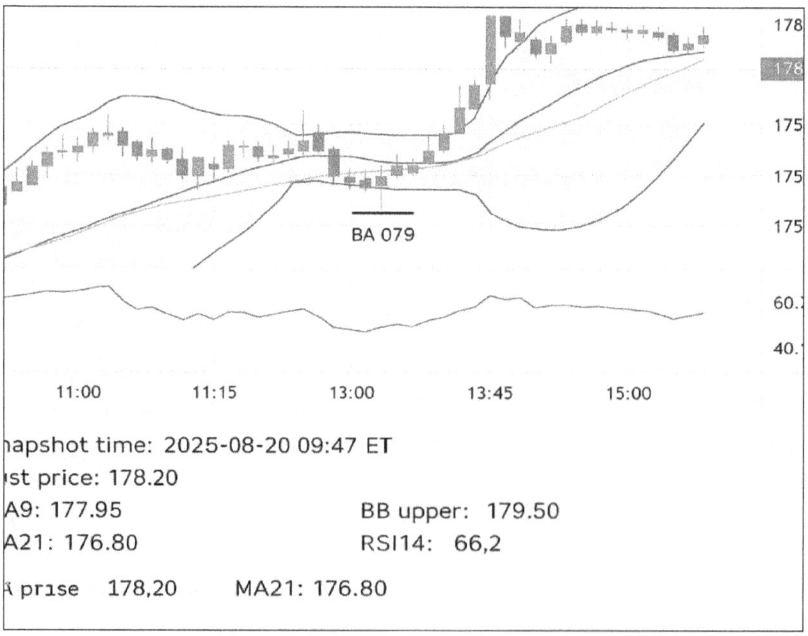

Fig 2.13 ChatGPT Chart Output (5Mins Candle Chart_EMA_BB_RSI)

If anything's missing from the image or caption, don't waste your time guessing. You need to simply just ask as below:

```
Return a one-line table: time, last price, MA9, MA21, BB
upper, BB lower, RSI14.
```

It wil give you a table that reads the following data as asked in the prompt:

Snapshot time	**2025-08-20 09:47 ET**
Last price	178.2
MA9	177.95
MA21	176.8
BB upper	179.5
BB lower	175.6
RSI14	66.2

Need Candle-Specific Data?

If you want to zoom in on one candle, then write it as:

```
From the snapshot timestamp, return the OHLC for the most
recent five minute candle and show MA9 and MA21 at that candle
close. Output a table with those fields.
```

It will output the following data:

Snapshot time	**2025-08-20 09:47 ET**
Last price	178.2
MA9	177.95
MA21	176.8

RSI14	66.2

Validate Breakouts

Now, while you try to validate a breakout, you need to look beyond the candle. You can try the following prompt:

```
On the snapshot, calculate BB width and compare current volume
to the 20 bar average. Return BB width and a yes or no for
volume confirmation where volume > 1.5x avg.
```

This prompt will give a clear, compact answer like the following table:

Snapshot time	**2025-08-20 09:47 ET**
BB width	3.90 (179.50 - 175.60)
Volume	320,000
20-bar average volume	200,000
Volume confirmation	Yes (1.6x avg)

Watchlists and Symbol Rotation

The traders generally spend more time inside the watchlist than any other panel. For traders, it is a group of shortlists of live possibilities and the heart of a fast workflow. That is why you learn to rotate through a list in a single prompt, pull top movers by volume or percent change, and pin tickers for deeper review. When you make these tasks repeatable you stop hunting for trades and start operating a clean, repeatable cycle which is basically the scan, confirm, and inspect.

So, to begin with, we start to create a watchlist that reflects your focus and we keep it small at first, like a core of ten to twenty tickers you trade well and a second list for new ideas, and then label the lists so they are easy to reference in a prompt. For example, we name one list as "Core Tech" and another "Morning Scan." The clearer the names, the easier it becomes to tell ChatGPT which list to read. In practice you will ask ChatGPT to rotate through the list and return ranked signals: top by percent change, top by unusual volume, and any ticker that crossed a key level.

Following is a quick single prompt that does all three and saves you several clicks.

```
Use TradingView watchlist "Morning Scan". For each ticker in
the list, return: symbol, percent change since yesterday
close, current volume and volume ratio to 20 bar average, last
price, and a one line catalyst if available. Then rank the
tickers by percent change and return the top five. Also
include a column that pins any ticker where volume ratio >
1.5. Return results as a table.
```

Now here, when the ChatGPT returns results, you will see a table titled as "Top 5 movers from Morning Scan" and it is something like the following:

Symbol	%Change	LastPrice	Volume	VolRatio	Catalyst	Pin
AAPL	+3.2%	178.20	1.1M	1.8	Earnings beat	YES
TSLA	+2.7%	124.50	820k	2.1	Analyst upgrade	YES
NVDA	+4.1%	412.75	950k	1.6	Sector tailwind	YES
MSFT	+1.9%	338.10	600k	1.0	None	NO
AMZN	+1.5%	172.50	500k	0.9	None	NO

The table above is your fast map. You will need to copy the pinned tickers into a short list for immediate review. The pin column is useful because it marks names that pass both the momentum and participation filters. If you want to keep the workflow entirely in ChatGPT, you can ask it to create a pinned group in the session memory. Usually, you will mirror that in TradingView by actually pinning or starring the tickers so the visual watchlist matches the GPT output.

Then, after the rotation and the initial ranking, you will do a more in-depth review of the pinned names. You will need to use a prompt that requests OHLC, moving averages, RSI value, Bollinger Band levels, and a note on whether the last bar has volume confirmation as shown below:

```
For the pinned tickers AAPL TSLA NVDA, provide the latest five
minute OHLC, last price, MA9, MA21, RSI14, BB upper, BB lower,
and a volume flag where volume > 1.5 x 20 bar average.Output
as a table with one row per ticker.
```

The immediate response you will get is the following table:

Symbol	Time	Open	High	Low	Close	Last	MA9	MA21	RSI14	BBupper	BBlower	VolFlag
AAPL	09:45	177.0	178.5	176.9	178.2	178.2	177.95	176.80	66.2	179.50	175.60	YES
TSLA	09:45	122.5	125.0	122.0	124.5	124.5	123.80	121.90	63.1	126.00	120.50	YES
NVDA	09:45	410.0	413.5	409.0	412.7	412.7	411.10	409.20	69.0	415.00	405.50	YES

These numbers in the above table give you the exact figures you need to put a plan together: entries, stops, and targets. The prompt asks for specific indicators and a clear volume rule. You will also want to pull top movers by specific filters across a broader universe for which we use the screener feature in TradingView and send the request to ChatGPT by naming the universe and the filter. And this is easily doable for which we simply ask for the top ten Nasdaq stocks by volume increase over the last thirty minutes or the top ten by percent change in the last hour as shown in the following prompt:

```
Scan NASDAQ for the top ten stocks by volume increase over the
last 30 minutes. For each, return symbol, percent change,
current price, 30 minute volume, and ratio versus the 20
period average. Return a ranked table.
```

This will give an immediate result as below:

Symbol	%Change	Price	Vol30m	VolRatio
AAA	+12.5%	15.40	2.5M	5.2

BBB	+9.2%	22.10	1.8M	4.1
CCC	-5.0%	8.30	1.6M	3.8

And finally, at the pre-market, you run one rotation prompt on your morning list. When the market opens, you run another rotation using the same list, but with intraday filters. Around midday, you will run the rotation with a prompt that only returns deltas since the last run. When you're done, you will see an archive prompt pop up. This stores the day's rotations, pinned lists, and closing moves so you can see which scans led to follow-through.

```
Archive today's Morning Scan results. Save table of top five
movers, pinned tickers, and closing price for each. And, then
label the archive with today's date.
```

This will archive the morning scan results and it will show as:

```
2025-08-20 Morning Scan Archive

Top5: AAPL TSLA NVDA MSFT AMZN

Pinned: AAPL TSLA NVDA

Close: AAPL 182.00 TSLA 125.50 NVDA 418.20
```

This above is how you make a watchlist work for you: rotate, rank, pin, and archive.

Summary

This entire chapter gives you a clear routine for working with TradingView and ChatGPT that keeps your desk fast and focused. First, you set up SuperCharts as your main canvas, build watchlists that reflect your strategy, and learn where the Pine editor fits without having to program. You got the charts lined up by venue time, turned on premarket and after-hours, picked execution and context intervals, and set rolling lookbacks so the screen only shows the recent bars that matter. And you learned to read candles by looking at OHLC, overlaying moving averages, RSI, and Bollinger Bands, and asking for annotated snapshots that return numeric captions instead of forcing you to guess from pixels.

This chapter is all about getting the prompts right so you can rotate a list, rank movers by percent and volume, pin candidates for deeper review, and archive daily scans for later benchmarking. You can use this foundation to cut latency, reduce noise, and trade from a disciplined, repeatable workflow.

CHAPTER 3: NEWS, SENTIMENT, AND CALENDAR SIGNALS

Buzzing Headlines

You know how a single headline can reroute a tape in seconds and change a day from trending to choppy. The market reacts only to a small fraction of what appears in the feed. Your job is to spot those items that alter cash flow expectations, sector outlooks, or risk appetite and to ignore everything else. Company level news like earnings surprises or regulatory approvals change fundamentals and cause immediate flows. Sector level items such as supply chain disruptions or analyst upgrades move groups of stocks together. Policy shifts from central banks or fiscal announcements change the backdrop and reweight which sectors perform. Political events create risk on or risk off moves that translate into gap opens and range expansions. Social chatter can hint at early momentum but it rarely replaces a verified catalyst. You want a system that surfaces price sensitive headlines fast and packages them so you can act without reading long articles.

Finance & Economic-specific GPTs

Within ChatGPT, specialized GPTs exist that deliver curated, trade ready analysis rather than general responses. These GPTs aggregate feeds, tag items by impact, and format outputs so you can read a short table and decide. We will connect one such model: **Finance & Economics - Stock, Crypto, Trade, Invest** by finllms.com. This is very helpful for day traders to pull price sensitive headlines and one line catalysts targeted to intraday decisions. We can ask the finllms GPT to filter by sector, recency, and estimated impact so your results stay concise. The GPT should return the items with a one-line catalyst and a three-word action cue. Just remember, when it comes to numeric sentiment scores, don't use them as a trade trigger, use them to prioritize. You will mostly be relying on the short catalyst, source, and time. That way, you can check the price and volume right away on TradingView or with your broker.

Now to locate it:

- Look for the GPTs menu in the left sidebar labeled GPTs or click Explore GPTs at the top of the page.
- If you do not see either option, open the menu and select Explore or More to reveal it.
- Then try typing 'finllms' or the full title 'Finance & Economics - Stock, Crypto, Trade, invest' into the search box and press Enter.
- This will open on the same window and its ready for use without any logins or further connectors.

But before you start using it regularly, it's a good idea to run a few quick checks before building any routines on top of the feed. So, ask the GPT for a recent five-minute OHLC row for a symbol, and then compare it to your market feed. Have the GPT return headlines with timestamps and source labels, and then confirm those items on the publisher page. If the GPT doesn't know the answer, it should reply with "unknown" or "refuse" when the live data isn't available. These checks are super quick, and they stop you from trusting unreliable inputs.

Asking Price Sensitive Headlines

Here, you will write prompts that name the trading universe, the sector, the recency window, and the output format. Be clear about what you want returned and how you want it formatted. Keep the output compact so you can scan it in seconds. Ask for a ranked list of headlines, a one-liner catalyst for each, and a three-word recommended action. The action is basically just a suggestion, like "check pre-market," "watch for breakout," or "wait for close." It's not a trade order. This way, you will have the power to make decisions and be able to act quickly.

You can try using the following prompt:

```
Use Finance & Economics Stock Crypto Trade Invest by
finllms.com. Scan the Nasdaq technology sector for headlines
from the last 60 minutes. Return the top five items ranked by
estimated price impact. For each item provide: symbol if
applicable, one line catalyst, timestamp, source, and a
recommended action phrase of up to three words. Output as a
compact table.
```

You will a table 'Top five Nasdaq tech headlines last 60 minutes' which is something like this:

Symbol	**Catalyst**	**Time**	**Source**	**Action**
NVDA	Guidance raised implying stronger near term AI chip demand	09:22 ET	Bloomberg	Check pre market
AAPL	Supply note reduces iPhone build estimates this quarter	09:15 ET	Reuters	Watch for gap
AMZN	Logistics partnership announced with major retailer	09:10 ET	PR Newswire	Watch breakout

TSLA	Regulator reports minor probe into recent software update	08:57 ET	Local newswire	Wait for close
MSFT	Large cloud contract won with governmental agency	08:50 ET	Company release	Check pre market

Now here, if an item looks important, try to confirm the source, price, and volume before you trade. And my personal advice is that this prompt should be running early in the day and then again around lunchtime for better trading tips. If you are an aggressive trader, then I will recommend running this prompt every 90 minutes during the trading session.

Filter by Sector and Recency

It's best to avoid broad scans that create noise. To get the most out of your research, narrow your query to a sector that matches your playbook and pick a recency window that fits your horizon. For scalps, aim for thirty minutes. If you're dealing with some pretty big intraday swings, try using the 60–120-minute range. If you combine the news filter with price or volume filters, the GPT will prioritize items that already show market reaction. That means the headline is more likely to lead to tradable moves instead of just idle chatter.

Below is an example prompt for the sector and recency:

```
Use Finance & Economics Stock Crypto Trade Invest by
finllms.com. Scan the semiconductor sector for headlines in
the last 30 minutes that are paired with at least a one
percent price move. Return symbol, one line catalyst, price
change, timestamp, and source in a table.
```

And the output should give you a table on semiconductor headlines with last 30 minutes price move as shown below:

Symbol	**Catalyst**	**PriceChange**	**Time**	**Source**

AMD	Strong gaming revenue preview	+2.3	09:28 ET	CNBC
NVDA	Analyst upgrade citing AI demand	+1.9	09:26 ET	Bloomberg
QRVO	Supplier flags component tightness	+1.2	09:20 ET	Company release

I suggest using those results as the top of your morning list. It shows both catalyst and market conviction.

Skip Long Reads for Short Catalysts

Also, when you're trading, ask for one line catalysts built as facts, plus the immediate price implication. Have the GPT label events as primary, like an earnings surprise, or secondary, like an analyst mentioned. You should give more weight to primary events and keep secondary items as watchlist material. If you can keep each catalyst to under fifteen words, that'll help the table stay readable.

Just use the following prompt:

```
For these tickers provide a one line catalyst that states the
primary event and the immediate implication for price. Keep
each entry to under fifteen words. Return as symbol followed
by one line catalyst.
```

It should answer you:

Symbol	**Catalyst**
NVDA	Guidance raised implies stronger near term AI chip demand
AAPL	Reduced iPhone builds signal potential revenue pressure this quarter

AMZN	Major retailer tie in could boost logistics revenue near term

You then add these one-line summaries to your scan table so you can see them whenever you desire to.

Prevent Sentimental and Social Noise

I'd suggest using sentiment as an early flag rather than a primary trigger. The GPT can pull social mentions and calculate a basic score. When the score spikes, just ask the GPT to show the top mentions and their sources. If we get some solid sources to back this up, bump the ticker up in your review order. If there's a lot of social chatter with no verified source, mark it as rumor and wait for confirmation. This discipline helps you avoid emotional decisions that might not serve your best interests.

A good example of the sentiment is as below:

```
Use Finance & Economics Stock Crypto Trade Invest by
finllms.com. For tickers AAPL TSLA NVDA return a sentiment
score for the last 30 minutes plus the top two mentions that
drove the score. Label each mention with source and timestamp.
```

This will yield you as:

Symbol	Sentiment	Top Mention 1	Time 1	Top Mention 2	Time 2
AAPL	0.21	Reuters	09:15	Reddit	09:10
TSLA	0.62	Twitter	09:18	Local news	09:05
NVDA	0.79	Bloomberg	09:22	Twitter	09:21

Now here, you can treat the score as a way to allocate attention and not as a trigger to trade. You must remember this...stick to your heart this thing.

Sentiment Scoring for Action

In our work, we see sentiment as a measured input, not as an emotion. We're looking for three simple numbers from the chatter window:

1. **polarity**, which tells us if the mentions are leaning positive or negative;
2. **strength**, which tells us how concentrated that bias is; and
3. **source variety**, which tells us if the buzz is coming from a lot of independent outlets or just one echo chamber.

These three values help us figure out where to put our attention, make sure our prices are in line, and decide if we should follow the crowd or go against the grain. I have break down the formulas into bite-sized pieces so we can do the math live at the desk or ask the GPT to compute them for us.

Collect Mentions

Open a session with the finllms GPT and ask for every mention in the last N hours where N equals 2, 4, or 6 depending on your horizon. And if you need a compact table with the timestamp, host name, 8-word excerpt, polarity label (positive, neutral, or negative), and confidence score (between 0 and 1), go full-on with the GPT. Just don't ask for the whole shebang or a long URL. The prompt has to force short excerpts and host names so the result fits on one screen.

It should be:

```
Use Finance & Economics - Stock, Crypto, Trade, Invest by
finllms.com.

For SYMBOL gather mentions in the last N hours.

Return rows: timestamp, host, excerpt (max 8 words), polarity
(positive/neutral/negative), confidence (0-1).

If live data unavailable reply unknown.
```

This will give you a tight table you can scan in seconds as shown below:

Time	Host	Excerpt	Polarity	Conf
21/08/25 9:35	Bloomberg	company raises guidance sharply	positive	0.93
21/08/25 9:42	Twitter	meme thread on product leak	positive	0.54
21/08/25 9:48	Reddit	rumor of supply cut	negative	0.6
21/08/25 9:58	CNBC	analyst raises target	positive	0.8

21/08/25 10:05	LocalBlog	echo of unverified rumor	negative	0.4
21/08/25 10:16	CompanyPR	announces logistics partnership	positive	0.88

If you want the GPT to compute metrics next, you can ask it to hold the table and return the aggregates as a second block as shown below:

polarity_mean	polarity_std	strength	source_variety
-0.023	0.147	0.02	6

Convert Words to Metrics

Next, we will convert the polarity labels into numbers: positive = +1, neutral = 0, negative = -1. To find the polarity, just take the average of those numbers across the window. And to figure out strength, just take the absolute value of that average and multiply it by something like (1 − normalized standard deviation). This way, if you've got a bunch of similar mentions, they'll score higher than random weak ones. We can calculate source variety as the number of unique host names and flag low variety when a small set of hosts (for example, 1–3) contribute the most mentions.

We will do a quick calculation to illustrate what I mean.

- Mention labels: [+1, +1, 0, +1, −1, +1, +1, 0, +1, 0]
- Polarity = mean = 0.45
- Strength = abs(mean) × consistency = 0.63 (example)
- Source variety = 5 distinct hosts

Get the above formulas in a spreadsheet or ask the GPT to return these three numbers so you do not have to calculate when you are in between the trading session.

Fetch Matching Price Series and Timestamps

Then, get OHLCV for the same symbol and the same time window using a five minute or fifteen-minute interval. You can also figure out the price direction as a percent change from the start of the window to the end, and you can calculate a short momentum metric like the change in VWAP or a linear slope of the recent closes. And just to be sure, make sure every timestamp lines up so that the clusters match up with the price bars in the same minutes. If the GPT can't get the price in the same session, just copy the mention table into your market tool and pull the price rows there.

Following is a prompt to fetch price rows:

```
Return OHLCV for SYMBOL from t_start to t_end at 5 minute
intervals. Label timestamps in ET. If live data unavailable
reply unknown.
```

Compare Sentiment vs. Price

If you put polarity and price returns on the same timeline, you will see what I mean. A dual axis line chart or a compact table that lists minute-by-minute polarity and minute-by-minute return would work well. Then, calculate a basic correlation coefficient across the window.

There are a few heuristics you can remember on the desk:

- polarity > 0.4,
- strength > 0.6, and
- source variety ≥ 5.

If these are met, it suggests a meaningful signal worth watching for continuation. If polarity is more than 0.4 but price moves lower, mark the setup as divergence and approach it with a defensive or contrarian plan. You can read it quickly as:

- Polarity 0.45 is a mild bullish lean.
- We're seeing consistent mentions of 0.63.
- Source variety 5 is all about a broad spread.
- The price changed by 1.8%, which means it's now over the threshold.

If most of the metrics are in line, go ahead and treat this as confirmation for your momentum plans. If they split, wait or fade, depending on your rules.

Prompts and Real Workflow

You can use the following template and then accordingly you can act upon the respective results:

```
Use Finance & Economics - Stock, Crypto, Trade, Invest by
finllms.com.

For SYMBOL collect mentions in the last N hours. Return
mention table (timestamp, host, excerpt, polarity,
confidence).

Then compute and return: polarity average, strength metric,
and source variety.
```

```
If live data unavailable reply unknown.
```

The result will be something like:

```
Mentions 10 rows Window 4h
09:12 Bloomberg Company raises guidance positive 0.93
09:20 Twitter Meme thread on product leak positive 0.54
09:25 Reddit Rumor of supply cut negative 0.60
09:30 CNBC Analyst raises target positive 0.80
09:41 LocalBlog Echo of rumor negative 0.40
Aggregated Polarity 0.45 Strength 0.63 Source variety 5 hosts
```

Then fetch price rows for the same window and compute correlation. If correlation is positive and metrics pass thresholds you escalate to a prewritten plan.

After all this, I recommend that you use the following checklist so you do not overthink:

- If polarity positive, strength high, source variety high, and price rising = alignment. Here, you may consider the momentum entry with defined entry, stop, target.
- If polarity positive, but strength low or variety low, and price flat or down = weak signal. I recommend here to wait for the confirmation or plan a fade if you trade contrarian.
- If polarity negative and price drops = confirmed weakness. Here, you must think for the short follow through setups with tight risk.
- If polarity negative while price rises = divergence. This is a strong alert to tighten the stops and wait for reversal triggers.

There are a few key things to keep in mind. When it comes to trading, treat sentiment as a helpful input, not as a set command. Put together an archive of every mention table and the matched price series so you can backtest which sentiment patterns led to follow through for your strategy. If you keep the rules simple, repeatable, and measurable, you will cut out most of the noise from all the social chatter.

Economic and Event Calendars

Usually, we trade around time-boxed events because those entries often create predictable periods of volatility. Things like economic reports, corporate earnings, central bank statements, and major political announcements can change liquidity and tilt market structure before price moves begin. You want a calendar that shows events by region, importance, and asset class. That way, we can start our morning routine with a clear map of what can move markets and when. So in this topic, we will try to find those events quickly, how to link every prompt to your local clock, and how to set practical pre-event buffers so you can plan for the move instead of just reacting to it.

Event Prioritization

Not every scheduled item matters equally. We prioritize events that directly influence intraday flow.

- The primary events carry immediate and measurable market impact, and you will treat them as the highest priority. News releases like GDP releases, non farm payrolls, headline inflation prints such as CPI, central bank policy rate decisions and accompanying statements, major corporate earnings and guidance revisions, large merger and acquisition announcements, and urgent regulatory approvals or rejections for key products, are all primary and considered to be major events.
- The secondary events influence market direction but usually require confirmation or follow up before they become tradable. These include sector specific reports, large industry conferences and keynote presentations, scheduled central bank speeches that do not announce policy, major regulatory filings that reveal long term change, and sizable analyst upgrades or downgrades.
- And the tertiary items create noise and only rarely drive sustained moves unless they amplify a primary event such as the opinion pieces, social media rumors, niche blog posts, celebrity mentions, and isolated forum chatter.

And don't forget to label each event as primary, secondary, or tertiary so your scans can weigh them right and so you can set pre-event buffers and position rules that reflect the likely impact.

Organizing Events

When it comes to the time windows, we will group events by region so you can see which ones are most at risk. The usual groupings are the United States, Europe, Asia Pacific, and Emerging Markets. Go ahead and pair each region with the relevant asset classes, like equities, fixed income, currencies, and commodities. For example, when US inflation prints affect US large caps, US treasury yields, and the US dollar, that has an impact on the market. A report on China's industrial production can impact the demand for Asia Pacific equities and commodities. When you organize events this way, you will have a short list to watch, instead of getting flooded with items that don't affect your selected instruments.

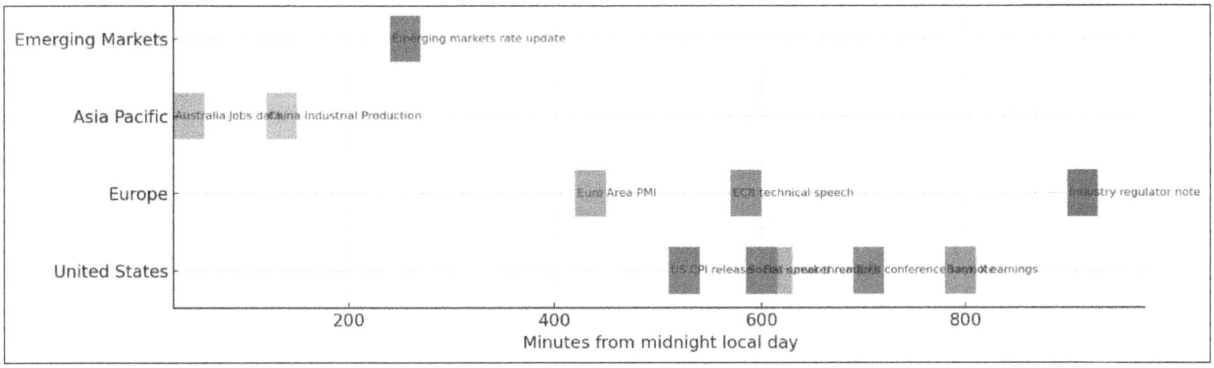

Fig 3.1 Grouped Event Timeline

In the above, the horizontal bars show events across a single trading day grouped by region. Each bar is a 30-minute window centered on the event time so you can see where regional clusters fall. Read the vertical axis to find the region and read left to right to see the time of day. If several bars sit close together you get a clear signal that multiple regions or asset classes will compete for liquidity during that interval.

Impact Scale

First, make a three-level importance scale: high, medium, and low. We suggest assigning high values to items that have historically moved the asset by significant amounts during the day, like central bank rate decisions or headline CPI prints. You can assign medium to items that sometimes move markets, like regional PMI or large company earnings. If an item doesn't usually create intraday volatility in your universe, assign it a low rating. If you keep a short note about the typical impact, it'll help you prioritize when you're swamped.

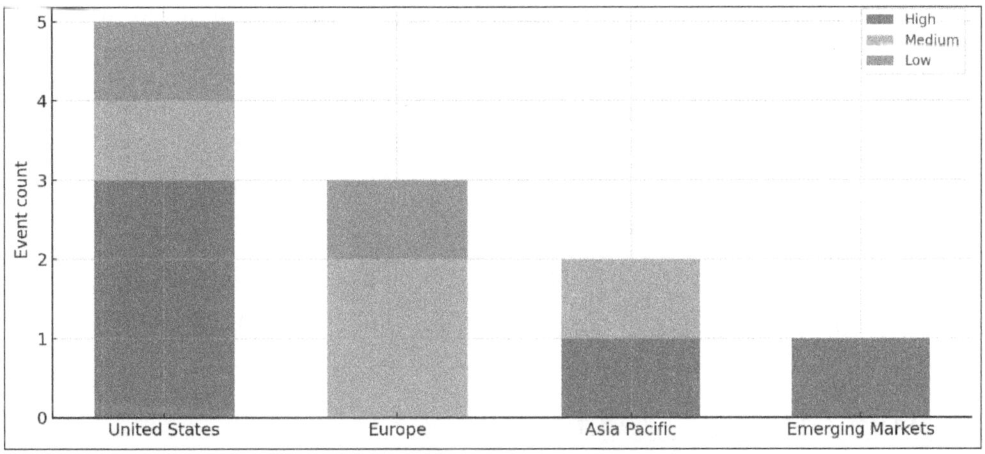

Fig 3.2 Event Counts Region-wise

In the above, the stacked bars show how many high medium and low importance events fall in each region for the sample day. The top of each stack shows the total event load for the region.

Use this to prioritize which session overlap to respect and where to tighten risk before the open.

Querying Time-Boxed Events

We can ask the GPT to give us an ordered list with the event time, local time, impact label, and affected asset classes. You can name the region and the window you care about, and request only events marked high or medium, unless you want full coverage. If you could get the GPT to include a one-line summary of why the event matters in terms of price drivers and to attach the event source, that'd be great.

The prompt we can run now is:

```
Use Finance & Economics - Stock, Crypto, Trade, Invest by
finllms.com. For the next trading day list all scheduled
economic and corporate events for the United States and
Europe. For each event return: UTC time, local time in my
location, region, importance (high medium low), affected asset
classes (equities bonds FX commodities), and a one line price
driver summary. Return results ordered by UTC time.
```

And the expected output will be:

Time (UTC)	**Time (ET)**	**Region**	**Impact**	**Assets Affected**	**Event / Notes**
07:30	03:30	United States	High	Equities, Bonds, FX	US CPI headline inflation print. Expect dollar strength and higher yields if above consensus.
12:00	08:00	Europe	Medium	Equities	Euro area PMI; affects European cyclicals and risk appetite.
14:00	10:00	United States	High	Equities	Major bank earnings; potential sector rotation on guidance.

Prompt Anchoring to Local Time

As long as you specify the local time you want in the prompt, you're all set. This avoids confusion when events roll across midnight boundaries and when platforms report in UTC. If you're trading from India, please use India Standard Time (IST) or the local time there. If you're trading from

New York, just use US Eastern Time (or ET). The GPT should give you both the UTC timestamp and your local timestamp, so you don't have to convert on the fly.

Following is an example to anchor time:

```
Provide the events in UTC and convert each event time to India
Standard Time IST. Return both times and label each row
accordingly.
```

And the expected table would be like:

Time (UTC)	Time (IST)	Region	Importance	Asset Classes	Event / Notes
07:30	13:00	United States	High	Equities, Bonds, FX	US CPI headline inflation print. Expect dollar strength and higher yields if above consensus.
12:00	17:30	Europe	Medium	Equities	Euro area PMI; affects European cyclicals and risk appetite.
14:00	19:30	United States	High	Equities	Major bank earnings; potential sector rotation on guidance.

With this, you can cross check times and impact with a single eyelook.

Setting Pre-Event Buffers

We usually say that a pre-event buffer is the number of minutes before a scheduled event when we stop taking on new risk or reduce position size. You can choose the length of the buffer based on how important the event is. If it's a high-importance event, use 20 to 30 minutes. For medium events, use 10 to 15 minutes. For low-importance events, use 0 to 5 minutes. The buffer gives us time to close out some of our more fragile positions, reduce our exposure, or move to cash before the expected volatility window opens. This simple guardrail keeps us from getting caught on the wrong side by sudden spikes and gives us a chance to confirm the price and volume before deciding whether to jump back in.

The following is how we request the buffers in a prompt:

```
For each listed event add a pre event buffer in minutes based
on importance. Use 30 minutes for High 15 minutes for Medium
and 5 minutes for Low. Return a column called pre buffer and a
column called cash advised true or false based on whether we
should reduce size to zero before the event.
```

And the shown below is how the buffers are applied by the GPT:

Event	Time (UTC)	Time (ET)	Importance	Pre-buffer (min)	Cash Advised
US CPI	07:30	03:30	High	30	True
Earnings Bank X	14:00	10:00	High	30	Depends on exposure to the sector
Euro PMI	12:00	08:00	Medium	15	False

Integrate Event Calendars

As a change, we will be merging the event feed into the morning rotation. The first thing to do is to focus on the most important items, and then check those tickers or sectors in your watchlist rotation. If an event affects a bunch of ticket holders, go ahead and pin them for the pre-event window. If a ticker has a pinned event, the rotation prompt should put active entries into that ticker on the back burner during the pre-buffer, unless you have a clear plan. This helps you avoid getting caught off guard by a headline you didn't see coming.

Following is the general prompt for it:

Use the "Morning Scan" watchlist. For each ticker return whether it has an event within its pre buffer window. If yes flag it as pinned and list event details. Return the watchlist table with an event flag column.

You will also mark session edges where one region closes and another opens. For example, US market open often aligns with European session close. That overlap window boosts liquidity but also raises the chance that a major event in either region will move global risk assets. Identify those overlapping windows in your morning routine and lower your guard threshold or reduce size if multiple high importance items stack up at the same time.

To sum it up, we've got to include a daily calendar screenshot with events color coded by importance, a table that shows UTC and local times, a sample watchlist with pinned event flags, and a flowchart that shows how to apply pre buffers to positions. These visuals will make the routine repeatable for you and anyone who follows your desk. Also, it's important to keep pre-event buffers at a minimum when you trade large and allow smaller buffers when you scalp small positions. Keep track of every event and outcome so you can see which event types lead to the most intraday moves for your style. Eventually, you will get the hang of adjusting the buffer sizes and importance scale so they match the real moves you see. That calibration makes a calendar into a handy risk control tool.

Earnings Windows without Fundamentals

Earnings and Price Behavior

Usually, we trade around earnings because the event puts a lot of unknowns into one moment. When an earnings report comes out, it changes how people expect revenue to be earned, how they think about the catalysts that drive it, and how they react to it. This often makes people in the market change their approach really quickly. Some stocks have a huge jump when they first open, while others are more stable.

The studies have shown that implied volatility jumps into earnings, then collapses after the print, and that realized moves sometimes outpace what economists and analysts expect. That kind of behavior creates both risk and opportunity for intraday players. Here, we're not so much into the fundamentals. We're more into the nitty-gritty of how to use ChatGPT and tell you when an earnings event is coming, how big a move the market expects, and how the stock's done after the last few earnings.

Upcoming Earnings

No matter what, we will always ask the GPT for the exact earnings timestamp and the exchange micro session label, like pre-market open, regular session, or after-hours close. The exact timestamp is important because it determines if you trade the print itself or if you wait for the first regular session bar. There are some companies that report before the market opens, and that often creates a gap that opens the day. With other companies, you have to wait until after the market closes to plan your trades for the day. So here, we will ask GPT to return the company symbol, the scheduled timestamp in UTC and your local time, the venue label, and a short note on whether the company typically reports before the open, after the close, or during the session. Also, there is something important about a one-line that says "Real-time confirmed". It is to indicate whether the source is the company press release or the exchange calendar as it prevents you from trading on a rumor by accident.

Expected Volatility Ranges and Implied Move Estimates

The GPT will be asked to get the implied volatility data and to figure out the expected move over the earnings window. You will need to match the earnings horizon with the option tenor. For example, use the nearest weekly or monthly option chain that covers the event. And when you're looking at the options, make sure you ask for at-the-money (ATM) implied volatility (IV), the expected move per share, and the percent expected move relative to the stock price. Also, ask the GPT to show you the historical realized move for the prior three earnings so you can compare the implied expectation to what actually happened. This will show if the market usually underestimates or overestimates moves for this name, and ultimately makes us better in choosing if we should trade on momentum or simply ignore.

Following is a quick prompt to try out:

```
For SYMBOL that reports on DATE return a compact numeric table
showing: option tenor label for the nearest chain, ATM IV for
that tenor, options implied expected move in dollars and
percent, realized day moves for the prior three earnings, and
a one line comparison and tactical cue from the set {prefer
momentum, prefer fade, avoid}. Refuse or reply unknown if live
data is unavailable.
```

Now here, you must ensure that you are using the so far used specialized GPT i.e. **Finance & Economics - Stock, Crypto, Trade, Invest** by finllms.com.

Now this prompt will yield the following output:

```
SYMBOL: ABC

Option tenor: Weekly 2025 08 28

ATM IV: 32.4%

Implied move: 2.40 USD   3.1%

Realized prior three: 1.8%   2.6%   4.0%

Comparison: Implied above historical average

Tactical cue: Wait for confirmation
```

If the options implied move materially exceeds the historical realized moves, then the market already expects a large swing and fading the print becomes risky. If the implied move sits below the historical realized moves, then the market underestimates risk and you may prefer a momentum plan after early confirmation.

Post Earnings Behavior

It'll be interesting to see how the stock did in the first trading day, the first week, and the first month after the last three earnings events. We need to get our hands on some numeric metrics that we can use right away. Following is what we're looking for:

- the gap direction and size expressed as a percentage,
- the end-of-day net change in percentage,
- the percentage of times the stock kept going in the same direction after the first session, and
- the intraday volatility expansion measured as the realized day range divided by the prior 20 bar average range.

If you could get the GPT to return a compact table with the columns titled **event_date, gap_open_pct, realized_day_range_pct, end_of_day_net_change_pct, follow_through_class**, and a brief note describing the typical post print path, it will be of immense use. We then simply have to take these numbers and use them to assign a style tag to the ticker. If the ticker shows repeated multi day trends, then tag it **trend_name** and prepare for extended exposure with a scaled exit plan. If the ticker tends to reverse intraday, then tag it **fade_name**.

Following is a quick example to put this into action:

```
For SYMBOL, summarize the last three earnings events. For each
event return: event_date, report_time (UTC and local),
gap_open_pct, realized_day_range_pct,
end_of_day_net_change_pct, follow_through_class
(continued/reversed/neutral), and brief_note (max 12 words).
After the table compute and return: follow_through_rate_pct,
average_gap_pct, average_realized_range_pct, and a style_tag
chosen from {trend_name, fade_name, neutral}. If live data
unavailable reply unknown.
```

The output window will be something like this:

```
SYMBOL: XYZ
```

EventDate	**ReportTimeUTC**		**Gap %**	**DayRange %**	**EOD %**	**FollowThrough**	**Note**
2025-05-05	12:30 UTC		+3.2	4.5	+2.8	continuation	Strong post print trend

2025-02-01	13:00 UTC		-1.1	3.8	-0.7	reversal	Bought then faded
2024-11-02	12:00 UTC		+0.9	2.1	+0.2	neutral	Small noisy move

```
And, the aggregates are:
follow_through_rate_pct: 33
average_gap_pct: 1.0
average_realized_range_pct: 3.47
style_tag: neutral
```

The above aggregates we have to convert them into a one-line mechanical rule for entries, stops, and targets. For example: if **style_tag** equals **trend_name** and **follow_through_rate_pct** is at least 66 then prefer momentum entries with a stop equal to half the **average_realized_range_pct** and a target equal to the **average_realized_range_pct**. If **style_tag** equals **fade_name** prefer fade setups with a stop above the high of the first regular session bar and a small profit target.

Volatility-Aware Prompts

The idea is that we will write prompts that request the event time, the options based on expected moves, recent realized moves, and the post earnings pattern, all in one call. Then, ask the GPT to return both numeric fields and a short recommendation phrase about which intraday plan suits the name given your stated risk rules. You can keep the recommendation as a tactical nudge, like "prefer momentum," "prefer fade," or "avoid for intraday." The prompt should be clear about not giving long explanations, and it should provide a short data table and a one-line tactical cue. Following is a sample prompt to run before the event:

```
For SYMBOL return: scheduled earnings timestamp in UTC and my
local time, venue label pre market regular session or after
hours, at the money implied volatility for the nearest option
tenor, options implied expected move in absolute and percent
terms, realized move for the prior three earnings with day and
7 day returns, and a one line tactical cue limited to two
words from the set prefer momentum prefer fade avoid. Return a
numeric table and refuse or reply unknown if data is
unavailable.
```

And the desirable output will be:

```
SYMBOL AAPL  Earnings 2025 08 29 12 30 UTC  08 00 ET  Venue
Pre market  ATM IV 28.5%  Expected move 3.20 USD  1.8%
Realized moves prior three 2.5% 1.9% 4.0%  Tactical cue prefer
momentum
```

Post-Event Risk Control

While we will be looking at the precise open bar OHLC for the session after printing the realized move versus the options-based expected move, we will also be measuring the intraday vol expansion as the realized intraday range divided by the prior average range. There will also be a short suggestion on stop distance expressed in cents or percent. The GPT won't set your stops for you, but they'll give you numbers you can use to choose an appropriate stop based on your account sizing rules. If the GPT can't find the live price, ask them to say "unknown" and just give the numeric fields so you can compare them quickly.

Following is a sample prompt to run after the event:

```
For SYMBOL after the earnings print return: first regular
session five minute OHLC bars from open to 10 30 ET realized
move versus options expected move intraday range divided by
prior 20 bar average and a recommended stop distance in
percent based on realized vol. Return numeric table only and
refuse if live data unavailable.
```

And the desirable output will be:

```
SYMBOL AAPL  First session 5m bars  09 30 100 103 99 102 Vol 1
200 000  Realized move 2.0%  Expected move 1.8%  Intraday vol
ratio 1.75  Suggested stop 1.0%
```

Now here, if the realized move exceeds the expected move and intraday vol ratio is above 1.5 you may accept a momentum entry that targets the measured move or a scaled profit taking plan. If realized move is below expected move and the post earnings pattern historically reverses you will prefer a fade with a tight stop above the high day.

Noise Control and Source Redundancy

With all the noise in the information ecosystem these days, the same piece of information is popping up on a bunch of different feeds, and low-credibility posts are making everyone feel like they need to act right away. When you clean the feed, it shortens the path from signal to action. What we're looking for is unique claims and independent confirmations from the top of our rotation. That way, we can tell whether price movements are driven by real capital or just amplified chatter.

Choosing News Pieces

The main anchors we will keep are things like original publisher items, exchange notices, regulatory filings, and block trade reports. These items give you proof of where they came from. We will be removing direct reposts that copy the same headline without checking the sources, anonymous social posts with no links, and duplicative feeds that only amplify a single origin. We will mark commentary pieces without primary evidence as tertiary. You won't be able to delete every social mention. When a scoop first appears, make sure to include one representative mention from each credible host and one social item. This gives you a wide view without getting cluttered, and it lets you spot early diffusion.

Following are the steps in the deduplication workflow you can run now:

- Go ahead and ask the GPT to bring back all the mentions from the last N hours that have these fields: timestamp, host, normalized_headline, excerpt, polarity, credibility, and link if they can find one.
- Just ask the GPT to normalize headlines by removing punctuation, lowercasing, and trimming trivial modifiers.
- Group mentions are sorted by normalized_headline, and we keep only the earliest mention plus up to two independent confirmations from different host domains.
- Mark the rest of the rows as duplicates and add a reason column that references the host we're keeping.
- Return a cleaned table of retained mentions and a provenance note listing which hosts confirmed the claim.

You can use this routine to make a reproducible, cleaned feed that you can archive and audit later.

Deduce Low Credibility Sources

It's pretty simple: if a publisher is well-known, they're more credible; if there's an author or a press release, that's even better; and if a host has been around for a while, that'll boost our credibility in the archive. Tag hosts as low, medium, or high. Don't remove mentions from low-credibility hosts, unless the item is exclusive and can't be confirmed elsewhere. When you see something that's not very credible, have your GPT look into it and label it as unverified if there's no proof. That step prevents rumor-driven panic without blocking real scoops that later prove to be true.

Cross-Check High Impact Claims

If a headline changes exposure a lot, you will need at least two independent confirmations and a direct link to the original source before you can take action. Just use a prompt that makes the GPT return unknown when it can't verify.

For example, to verify a high-impact claim, you can:

```
For the claim "<short normalized headline>" search the last 30
minutes and return: earliest host, earliest timestamp, up to
two independent confirmations with host and timestamp, and
direct link to the primary source (press release exchange
notice or regulator page). If you cannot find two independent
confirmations return UNKNOWN.
```

And, it will give us an output like:

```
Claim: Regulator approves product X

Earliest: 09:12 Bloomberg 09:12 ET
https://bloomberg.com/article

Confirmations:

1) Reuters 09:15 ET https://reuters.com/article

2) SEC notice 09:16 ET https://sec.gov/notice

Verification: CONFIRMED
```

If you don't have confirmations, don't trade size into the claim. The prompt above should be used as a hard gate before escalating to a larger size.

Sentiment Balancing

If you want to measure bias, ask the GPT to return both raw mention counts and unique host counts by polarity. You can see chatter volume with raw counts, and unique hosts show independent adoption. You can use both to see if a bias shows either broad adoption or concentrated amplification.

The following is the prompt to measure bias and deduplicate at the same time:

```
For SYMBOL collect mentions in the last N hours. Return for
each mention: timestamp host normalized_headline excerpt
polarity (positive/neutral/negative) credibility
(low/medium/high) and link if available. Then group by
normalized_headline keep first mention and up to two
confirmations from different host domains. Finally compute
counts: total_mentions unique_hosts bulls bears neutral
percent_bulls percent_bears and return the cleaned table plus
counts. If verification items are missing reply UNKNOWN.
```

This will give a table as desired:

Time	Host	Headline	Polarity	Cred	Link
09:12	Bloomberg	Regulator approves product X	Positive	High	https://bloomberg
09:15	Reuters	Regulator approval confirmed	Positive	High	https://reuters
09:20	Twitter	UserX claim no link	Positive	Low	UNKNOWN

And, it will also give more output as:

```
Counts: total_mentions 12  unique_hosts 5  bulls 8  bears 2
neutral 2  percent_bulls 66%  percent_bears 17%

Removed: 9 duplicates explained as reposts of Reuters
Bloomberg
```

You can use the counts as a sort of gate. For example, if the percent_bulls is over 60% and unique_hosts is more than 4, we should escalate to an immediate review. If percent_bulls is high but unique_hosts is low, treat the signal as amplification and wait for confirmations.

Summary

So, with this, we're all set. We've got a clear toolkit for using ChatGPT and the special GPT to make faster, cleaner intraday decisions. We figured out how to find headlines that might change based on price, and we started asking for timestamps, sources, and short explanations of what's going on so we can see signals next to price and volume. We worked on finding a finance-specific

GPT, doing quick OHLC checks, and anchoring prompts to our local clock so we don't lose minutes to time conversions. We set simple pre-event buffers to protect size and reduce surprise, and we translated options, implied moves, and past post-earnings behavior into plans that are aware of volatility. We measured sentiment using polarity, strength, and source variety, and then compared sentiment to price to decide between momentum and contrarian plans.

We came up with a way to deduplicate the data so we could get rid of duplicate posts, ignore low credibility hosts, and make sure everything was confirmed before we made any decisions. And we will make sure to archive all the outputs and outcomes so we can build up our confidence with the data. Remember to keep these steps numeric, repeatable, and fast so our desk trades with less noise and more clarity.

Chapter 4: High-Impact Prompt Crafting

Defining Role and Objective

We're always trying to trade off against time and noise. The prompts make ChatGPT super efficient because they narrow the range of possible answers and force outputs into actionable formats. It's been shown that when tasks are clearly defined, there's less back and forth and more responses with numeric fields like timestamps, price levels, and confidence scores. When a prompt names a persona, we use a single sentence to define the objective, scope, and format of the data. This helps us remove ambiguity and shape the GPT to return labeled tables and short, tactical cues instead of long commentary.

There are two practical benefits to this:

- First, you will get a usable result faster.
- Second, you will get structured fields that you can map directly to charts and orders.

It's like when traders spend ages clarifying a reply or chasing down some random idea without any real data to back it up. The prompts should be short and sweet so the GPT can give a concise table or a brief checklist, along with a one-liner that tells them what to do next and a target. When you're getting started with this process, think of it as part of the session. This way, the aide becomes a way to make decisions faster, not just a tool for generating text.

Setting 'Technical Strategist' Persona

When we open the first message, we will start with a personal touch and a clear goal in mind. The persona gives us a framework for tone and focus, and the objective tells ChatGPT what the decision role is. A persona named technical strategist signals that the GPT should think like a quant aware desk analyst who prefers numeric fields and concise tactics. The one-line objective tells the GPT the one thing we want to achieve in this session. For example, we will write a starting message that'll look like a short contract to the GPT. That way, there's no scope creep, and the output stays compact and repeatable. The persona should be short and stable throughout the session so that follow-up prompts can take the same role without having to restate it each time.

If you notice what happens when the persona is absent, you will see what I mean. The GPT will start with a lot of generalizations and often include long disclaimers. That prose feels smart, but it's just a waste of time and attention on a desk that needs numbers. This is called scope creep. It happens when the model assumes you want additional analyses like macro context or full fundamentals without asking if you want them. The result is a longer response and a shift away from tradable cues. If the output is vague, it usually doesn't include timestamps, price levels, or confidence scores. If a form has missing fields, you have to ask follow-up questions, and that costs time. We can avoid this by starting every relevant conversation with the persona and a one-line objective, and by requesting explicit output fields that we can use right away for entries, stops, and targets.

Simple and Precise Objective

When you're ready, go ahead and paste the two lines below as the first message of the session. The message lays out boundaries and the format the GPT has to follow. It also makes it clear that you're looking for a short numeric table and a quick tactical cue, not a long essay. Following is the simple prompt you can try out:

```
Persona Technical strategist with focus on intraday price
triggers and risk control. Provide a compact numeric table
that lists symbol time last price key levels and a one line
tactical cue mapped to an entry stop and a target. Return only
the table and the one line cue. If live data unavailable reply
UNKNOWN.
```

In addition, we will let the GPT know what columns we need, and how many rows we're looking for, so they can get the job done right. Also, be sure to name the timeframe, the venue, the exact interval, and the lookback so the returned bars match your chart. If the result depends on external headlines, ask for confidence or source columns. The demand should be brief and easy to work with. When you need to follow up, ask one clear question that references a row and a column from the previous table. This keeps the context tight and lets the GPT answer with just a few words. This pattern reduces cognitive switching and keeps the workflow fast.

Prompt Comparison

We will talk about two sample prompts below that you can use as templates. The first prompt shows how a vague request can lead to a long response that makes you want more specific details. The second prompt shows how the persona and the one-line objective force a compact table plus a tactical cue you can act on immediately. You can paste both templates into My GPT or your prompt library so you can recall them when you need them.

The vague prompt is something like this:

```
Scan tickers for possible intraday plays and tell me what
looks interesting.
```

Whereas, a tight prompt with well defined persona and objective is:

Persona Technical strategist with focus on intraday price triggers and risk control.

Objective Provide a compact numeric table that lists up to five symbols with columns: symbol time last_price premarket_high premarket_low MA9 MA21 RSI14 volume_volratio and a one line tactical cue mapped to an entry price stop and target. Scan NASDAQ tech universe for the last 90 minutes. Return only the numeric table and the one line cues. If data missing reply UNKNOWN.

We're expecting a compact table with clearly labeled columns. The table has to use the exact field names we asked for so we can map rows to the chart. There's a single line cue that comes after the table, and it uses short tags like "prefer momentum, prefer fade, avoid" so that your decision template can interpret the cue and figure out the entry sizing. It only takes a few seconds to verify. You will be checking the last price and the premarket high or low against TradingView. If you see a timestamp that doesn't match, just ask the GPT to adjust the times to match your local clock. If the GPT reports "**UNKNOWN**" for missing live data, the routine will stop instead of making up numbers. That rule is there to stop false confidence.

To the best of my experience with the ChatGPT, you must get the following table and one-line comment:

Symbol	**Time**	**Last Price**	**Premarket High**	**Premarket Low**	**MA9**	**MA21**	**RSI14**	**VolRatio**
NVDA	09:28	415.20	418.00	410.50	412.8	409.3	68.2	1.7
AAPL	09:28	178.20	179.50	175.60	177.9	176.8	66.2	1.5

```
One line tactical cues:
NVDA prefer momentum entry 416 stop 412 target 423
AAPL avoid
```

We must treat the persona and the one-line objective as a ritual before any meaningful prompt that supports trading decisions. The ritual reduces fluff and enforces repeatable outputs.

Precise Inputs

Clear and Precise Anchors

There are five inputs that we will treat as non-negotiable anchors for any prompt that wants a tradable output. These are:

- Ticker,
- Venue,

- Interval,
- lookback, and
- Indicators

If you can, be specific about each one so the GPT can match its data fetch and calculations to the exact bars you will see on your chart. Give the ticker the exchange prefix so there's no chance of loading the wrong instrument. Please name the venue as the market or data feed so the GPT uses the correct session rules and timestamps. You can name the interval as the candle size, like one minute, five minutes, or fifteen minutes. Then, name the lookback as the number of bars or minutes to analyze. Please name the indicators you want, including the exact parameters, such as MA9 or RSI14. When you see all five inputs in the first prompt, the GPT will give you numbers and levels that you can map directly to TradingView or your broker. This is pretty straightforward, and you won't need any more clarification.

Now, we will show how these anchors convert a vague ask into a short contract. You simply paste the following persona line followed by the first block:

```
Persona Technical strategist with focus on intraday price
triggers and risk control.

Objective Provide a compact numeric table for SYMBOL VENUE
INTERVAL LOOKBACK with columns: symbol time last_price
level_resistance level_support MA9 MA21 RSI14 VWAP
volume_volratio and a one line tactical cue mapped to an entry
stop and a target. Use exchange prefix in the symbol. Use
local time zone ET. If live data unavailable reply UNKNOWN.
```

And while you do this, please do not forget or atleast make a final check to ensure that the SYMBOL VENUE INTERVAL LOOKBACK are replaced with actual values. For example, let us say we want a five-minute scan of NASDAQ tech, then you will set NASDAQ: AAPL TradingView 5 minutes 180 bars. The GPT then returns precise numeric rows you can drop into the chart and trade from immediately. That short contract removes ambiguity and prevents the GPT from returning context heavy prose that wastes a precious minute or two.

Threshold as Decision Gates

Now we will introduce thresholds because numbers without decision gates remain words. A threshold is a numeric rule that signals a trade condition. Use thresholds for indicator break points for percent moves for volume spikes and for volatility expansion. Define absolute and relative thresholds so they match your style. Absolute thresholds work for indicators such as RSI14 above 70 or below 30. Relative thresholds work for price moves such as a percent change from the open greater than one percent or volume greater than three times average. Keep thresholds simple so you can mentally apply them during the session and so the GPT can compute them quickly.

Accurate Levels and Time Stamps

If you could get the GPT to send you the numeric levels and the exact time stamps for those levels, that'd be great. The time stamps let you align the mention to the exact candle. This prompt is for requesting thresholds and level values.

```
For SYMBOL at VENUE return: last_price, premarket_high,
premarket_low, MA9 value, MA21 value, RSI14 value, VWAP value,
volume over the lookback, average volume, and compute
thresholds: RSI_overbought 70 RSI_oversold 30
Volume_spike_threshold as 3x average and Price_move_threshold
as 1 percent from open. For each threshold return the exact
timestamp when the condition last tripped within the lookback.
Return a compact numeric table and a one line action cue. If
live data is not available return UNKNOWN.
```

The GPT will return values like MA9 equals 412.80 with the time stamp 09:28 and RSI14 equals 68.2 at 09:28 so you can place stops and entry triggers by the exact candle. You and I will not guess levels from a picture. We will request timestamps so the plan reads like a mechanical script rather than a narrative.

Live Sync

Next, we will put anchors and thresholds together to make a working procedure that you can run live. Run the first prompt to get levels and the second to compute thresholds. If the thresholds already meet your trade rules, bump the row up to the immediate review list. If the thresholds aren't meeting your rules, just keep the ticker in the watch bucket and rerun the prompts after the next N bars. For the N value, just use a simple number. For five-minute charts, use three bars, and for one-minute charts, use five bars. It's best to keep the loop short so you don't miss a quick breakout.

Composite Execution Prompt

Following is a single composite prompt that gathers anchors thresholds and produces a ready plan:

```
Persona Technical strategist with focus on intraday price
triggers and risk control.
```

Objective Provide a compact numeric execution plan for SYMBOL at VENUE using INTERVAL with LOOKBACK bars. Return columns: symbol time last_price entry_long entry_short stop_long stop_short target_long target_short MA9 MA21 RSI14 VWAP volume average_volume volume_ratio and timestamp_when_threshold_crossed. Compute two threshold conditions: price crossing above MA9 while volume_ratio >= 1.5 and RSI14 above 66. If threshold true fill entry_long with the next tick price rounded to two decimals and compute stop_long at entry minus 0.7 percent and target_long at entry plus 1.5 percent. Return only the numeric table and a one line tactical cue. If any live data is missing reply UNKNOWN.

The output it gives will be ready to act upon without extra calculations. The below could be the best output it will give:

Symbol	Time	Last Price	Entry Long	Entry Short	Stop Long	Stop Short	Target Long	Target Short	MA9	MA21	RSI14	VWAP	Volume	Avg Vol	Volume Ratio	Threshold Timestamp
NASDAQ: NVDA	09:28	415.20	416.00	NA	412.08	NA	422.24	NA	412.8	409.3	68.2	415.50	1,200,000	700,000	1.71	09:28

```
One line tactical cue:

NVDA prefer momentum entry 416 stop 412 target 423
```

Now, when you get such output, you need to verify the **last_price** and the **VWAP** in TradingView. If the numbers match, you will post a manual order with the entry stop and target from the plan. If the GPT returns **UNKNOWN,** then pause and run the verification prompts we taught earlier so you do not trade on invented numbers.

Over time, you will work on adjusting threshold numbers like volume multiples and percent moves so that the GPT aligns with your level of risk appetite. The outputs will become a mechanical trade plan that you can execute with minimal cognitive friction.

Output Format

There's not a lot of time to decide. If your response is easy to scan and maps directly to an order ticket, it'll reduce hesitation and error. The way things are shaped affects how people see them and how they act. A paragraph of prose forces reading and interpretation. A compact table points to the exact cells we need to verify. A short numbered plan gives us a set of easy steps to follow. The key is picking the shape that matches the decision moment. And use bullets when you need to do a quick check. Use compact tables when you need exact numbers and timestamps. When you've got a sequence to follow to enter or exit a trade, use numbered steps. These choices affect how long it takes to execute the trade and the quality of the trade.

Three Primary Shapes

Bullets for fast sense checks

The bulleted outputs list the most important items so you can scan in one eye sweep. These bullets help to list catalysts, to note quick caveats, or to summarize verification steps. You can rest each bullet to a single idea and include a numeric field when that idea depends on a number such as a percent move or a time as the goal is to let your eyes land quickly and then move to the chart.

Compact tables for direct mapping to chart

With tables, you can see the numbers in the labeled cells, so you can check the levels without having to convert them. And use tables to keep track of the last price, support and resistance, moving averages, and the exact candle timestamp when a threshold tripped. Also, make sure the names of your design columns match the chart fields. If you can keep the row count small, you will be able to read across and match cells to price action right away.

Numbered steps for action sequences

The numbered steps turn your analysis into a plan you can actually execute. You can use them to set entry triggers, stop placements, profit targets, and the order of verification. All steps have to be atomic, meaning each action can be executed or rejected without having to re-read the whole plan.

Request Shapes

After your persona and objective lines, paste one of these formats. They'll lock the GPT into the right shape so the output arrives in the right form at the moment you need it.

Bullets template

```
Return three bullets only. Each bullet contains a one line
catalyst and one numeric field. For example: Catalyst colon
one line; Numeric colon value and timestamp in ET. If data
unavailable reply UNKNOWN.
```

The output which it will generate will be as:

```
Catalyst colon Fed speaker mentions hawkish tone Numeric colon
09 colon 28 ET percent move 0.9

Catalyst colon Company X posts revenue surprise Numeric colon
09 colon 15 ET gap 2.4 percent

Catalyst colon Sector A shows volume spike Numeric colon 09
colon 22 ET volume ratio 2.1
```

After this, you sweep the bullets and pick the single item that requires immediate review. The bullets reduce reading time and preserve focus when multiple events compete.

Compact table template

```
Return a compact table with columns: symbol time last_price
support resistance MA9 MA21 RSI14 VWAP volume_avg and an
action column with one of prefer momentum prefer fade avoid.
Limit to five rows. Return numeric values only and timestamp
in ET. If data unavailable reply UNKNOWN.
```

Now here, the output you get is:

Symbol	Time	Last Price	Support	Resistance	MA9	MA21	RSI14	VWAP	Volume Avg	Action
NASDAQ: ABC	09:28	54.20	53.80	55.10	54.00	53.40	62.1	54.10	1,000,000	prefer momentum

Once you get this, you try to match the values to the chart cells and you place the order without further calculation. The timestamp tells you which candle to inspect and the action column gives a short cue you have pre defined.

Numbered steps template

```
Return a numbered list of steps to execute if condition X
triggers. Example step one verify last price matches
TradingView step two enter with limit price step three place
stop step four place target. Each step must be one line. If
data unavailable reply UNKNOWN.
```

This will give you the following output:

```
Verify last price 54.20 on TradingView at 09 colon 28 ET.

If price trades above resistance 55.10 enter long with limit
55.05.

Place stop at 53.80 and size to 1 percent of equity.

Plan to take partial profits at 56.00 and exit remainder at
57.50.
```

In this case, a trader who prefers mechanical execution follows the numbered list and avoids hesitation. These steps make it clear which ticket to send and which stop to place.

Combined Formats

If you ask me, a layered output would work better for us. You can start by making a list of potential candidates. Then, move on to a compact table to confirm the levels. And finally, add numbered steps for the selected candidate. This sequence helps you stay fast and doesn't make it so hard to switch between analyzing and executing.

We should try a composite template that gives us a short bullet list, a table, and a numbered action plan for the top candidate. For example:

```
Persona Technical strategist with focus on intraday price
triggers and risk control.

Objective Provide three bullets of top catalysts with
timestamps. Then return a compact table for the top symbol
with numeric levels and timestamps. Finally return a numbered
plan to execute if threshold conditions are met. Limit the
entire output to 30 lines. If data unavailable reply UNKNOWN.
```

The output that it will give will be something like this:

```
Catalyst, Company X revenue surprise 09: 15 ET gap 2.4 percent

Catalyst, Sector A volume spike, 09: 22 ET vol ratio 2.1
```

```
Catalyst, Fed speaker hawkish, 09: 28 ET percent 0.9
```

Symbol	Time	Last Price	Support	Resistance	MA9	MA21	RSI14	VWAP	Volume Avg	Action
NASDAQ: ABC	09:28	54.20	53.80	55.10	54.00	53.40	62.1	54.10	1,000,000	prefer momentum

```
Verify last price 54.20 on TradingView at 09 colon 28 ET
If price above 55.10 enter long limit 55.05
Stop 53.80 size 1 percent equity
Profit take partial 56.00 full 57.50
```

For each decision moment, decide on a shape and practice it until it becomes second nature. When you're following the layered sequence bullets table steps, you're basically following the lay of the land. Keep cues short and numeric so we can act with speed and clarity.

Trading Guardrails

We trade with numbers, timestamps, and source labels. The level of trust in these areas determines whether we open a position, reduce size, or step aside. If an GPT makes up a number, gives a quote to the wrong place, or makes up a timestamp, the desk can lose a lot of money before the mistake is found. If the data is good, you will be able to make decisions faster because you won't have to stress about the output.

There's one simple rule:

Any field that would change exposure has to have a source label and a timestamp

This rule makes the GPT connect analysis to things like exchange notices, company press releases, official regulator pages, or articles in named publications that can be checked out. If the GPT can't find a primary source, they should reply with a single-word unknown instead of making an educated guess. This discipline protects your investment and keeps your customers' trust.

Source Labels, Timestamps, and Uncertainty Markers

Our GPT will need to put a source label and an exact timestamp in each of the numeric fields. If you do that, make sure to put those requirements into the first lines of every session prompt so the GPT can't skip them. To get the price or volume, use the market feed name like TradingView or your broker feed. When you're picking headlines, try using publishers like Reuters, Bloomberg, and the SEC. And for derived fields like implied move or realized day range, just ask for the calculation timestamp and the source of the inputs. This'll help you figure out where a value came from, whether it was an option chain vendor, an exchange feed, or a news API. When the GPT returns a numeric table, you will need to scan the source column before scanning the numbers. Eventually, we will work together to figure out which hosts are always reliable and which ones need a little more checking.

For now, let's just treat unknown as a safety switch. The GPT has to return unknown in the following cases: when any live input is not available, when the chain of custody for a fact cannot be established, or when the timestamp mismatch cannot be reconciled. We need three explicit uncertainty markers in the output: unknown for missing data, low confidence when a source is unverified, and disputed when credible outlets conflict on a key fact. If you could include those markers as dedicated columns in the numeric table, that'd be great. That structure forces a rapid triage. And if the unknown flag pops up, you will want to pause and run verification prompts. It's all about reducing size and tightening stops if you're feeling a bit insecure. If a dispute comes up, just treat the claim as unresolved and focus on monitoring instead of sizing. These simple rules keep the GPT from making false claims that sound believable. They turn uncertainty into clear steps to take.

Writing Citation-backed Prompts

It's best to put the source requirement and the refusal rule into the persona block. When you're talking to an GPT, make sure they acknowledge the rule in their first reply. When you're writing, make sure to use clear language that doesn't allow for interpretation and includes direct links to the original sources. The short prompt below becomes the first message in any session where you will act on data.

Persona Technical strategist with an absolute no guess policy. Objective Return numeric tables only. For every numeric field include a source label and a timestamp. If the GPT cannot verify a numeric field from a primary source return UNKNOWN in that cell. Where a claim is reported by multiple credible hosts include up to two source links. Label any unverified social item low confidence and any conflicting claims disputed. Acknowledge these rules in one line and then await my symbol query.

Let us say you want to write a prompt which can have a headline that could change exposure materially. Now such a prompt demands two independent confirmations and direct links. Following is a sample prompt:

```
For the claim "<short normalized headline>" search the last 30
minutes and return: earliest host, earliest timestamp, up to
two independent confirmations with host and link, and a
verification status that is either CONFIRMED, DISPUTED, or
UNKNOWN. If CONFIRMED include the direct link to the primary
source. If UNKNOWN return UNKNOWN.
```

And then, the following is something you can expect which will have the headline prompt:

```
Claim: Regulator approves product X

Earliest: Bloomberg 09:12 ET https colon slash slash bloomberg
dot com slash article

Confirmations:

1) Reuters 09:15 ET https colon slash slash reuters dot com
slash article

2) SEC notice 09:16 ET https colon slash slash sec dot gov
slash notice

Verification: CONFIRMED
```

When the response returns UNKNOWN or shows only social posts you treat the claim as unverified and you do not change size. That rule prevents being first into an illusion and it keeps the archive clean for later analysis.

Call Source of Numeric Metrics

When you're working on the metrics, like implied move, realized day range, or intraday vol ratio, ask the GPT to bring back a provenance column for each. The provenance column is where you will find the input fields and sources for each one. That clear chain of custody makes it easy to audit the calculation. If the GPT can't say where the info came from, the provenance cell should read "UNKNOWN." You can use the sample template below for any derived metric you're going to act on.

```
For SYMBOL return numeric table with fields: last_price source
timestamp, implied_move dollars source timestamp,
realized_move percent source timestamp, intraday_vol_ratio
value source timestamp, and a provenance column listing the
inputs and their hosts. If any input is missing return UNKNOWN
for the derived field and mark provenance UNKNOWN.
```

Based on the above prompt, it will produce three different flags. If you see an unknown flag, you should stop and verify it. When you see a low confidence flag, you should reduce size and tighten stops. If there's a dispute over a flag, it's better to wait and see how it's resolved before adding risk. For example, if the implied move is there but the provenance says "social feed only," you might have low confidence, and you could cut your position size in half. If two credible regulators report different wording on an approval, then it looks like there's a dispute, and you don't trade size until a clarifying source posts, then that's how it is. When it comes to trading, remember that these markers are just part of the process, not obstacles to be avoided. Eventually, you will probably prefer prompts that give you fewer unknowns because your verification routines will have shown that they're reliable.

Audit, Archive, and Score the Sources

We will both keep track of every prompt output, the source links, and the actual price path that we follow. It'd be great if you could build a simple weekly scorecard that rates hosts based on accuracy and timeliness. Each host should have two fields: confirmation rate percent and average lead time in minutes relative to price moves. A high confirmation rate and positive lead time will move a host into your trusted list and reduce manual checks. If you get a low score, it'll put you in the "low confidence" bucket, and then it'll check you more in future prompts. That feedback loop basically turns the GPT from a black box into a measurable signal layer.

The following is the final prompt which you can ready-made paste it as it is:

```
Persona Technical strategist with an absolute no guess policy.
Objective Return a compact numeric table for SYMBOL with
columns: last_price source timestamp, premarket_high source
timestamp, MA9 value timestamp source, VWAP value timestamp
source, implied_move dollars source timestamp, provenance
inputs and hosts, and a verification flag per row that is
CONFIRMED DISPUTED or UNKNOWN. If any live data is missing
return UNKNOWN in the cell. Reply only with the table.

For SYMBOL check headlines in the last 60 minutes and return
cleaned mentions with fields: timestamp host
normalized_headline excerpt polarity credibility and link.
Group duplicates keep earliest plus up to two confirmations.
For any claim that would change exposure request at least two
primary links and mark verification CONFIRMED otherwise
UNKNOWN.
```

If we follow these rules, the GPT becomes a disciplined tool for the desk. It's all about trust, and trust is built through doing the same things over and over again and being willing to pause and ask questions when you don't know something. And remember to save every session and score your feeds until the trusted list gets smaller and the unknown column doesn't pop up as much.

Summary

So, with this chapter wrapping up, you've got a solid grasp on a set of tried-and-true prompt practices that make ChatGPT a real game-changer for trading, not just a source of random noise. It's all about starting sessions with a short, focused persona called the technical strategist and a one-line objective so everyone knows what to expect and responses stay on point. You got the hang of anchoring every prompt with a ticker, exchange prefix, venue, interval, lookback, and exact indicators, so the numbers on your chart line up directly. You defined thresholds for indicators like volume and price moves, so the GPT can compute decision gates and attach timestamps for exact candles.

We've learned to request outputs in shapes that match decisions, bullets for quick checks, compact tables for exact levels, and numbered steps for execution as this helps you trade faster and with less ambiguity. We also learned to request source labels, timestamps, and explicit uncertainty markers, and to force the GPT to return unknown when verification is not possible. Then, we should archive outputs, score sources, and tune thresholds over time. We can do this by confirming the rate and lead time. All these habits help you make decisions faster, reduce errors, and trade from verifiable signals.

CHAPTER 5: SENTIMENT AND VOLUME PATTERNS THAT MATTER

A lot of market moves are driven by the mix of narratives and capital. But sentiment shifts can change expectations, and when that happens, it affects the price. When there's a sudden surge in volume, it often means new info is hitting the market, which forces a quick reprice. It's usually the big orders that keep things going. Most of the time, moves based on social chatter aren't very deep. They might even backfire once the pros test out the claim. We should think of sentiment as a short-lived force with measurable decay, and treat volume as the validator of that force. If you read both parts carefully, you can react to price changes instead of just following trends.

Role of Social Mood

The way social mood works is that it takes a bunch of small reactions from people and puts them together to make one big signal. That signal shows up on feeds as bullish or bearish claims, and it speeds up when accounts are in sync. When prices go up fast, there's a higher chance that the first wave will reach levels that trigger automated actions, and then attract quick follow-up from traders who chase momentum. If there aren't any credible hosts or there isn't enough volume behind a wave, it makes the move fragile. It's best to think of social mood as a signal that changes over time instead of a permanent truth. You can measure that decay so the GPT can downweight older mentions and return a score that matches the desk's intuition about momentum at a given moment.

Social Mood Theories

There are two practical theories that determine the mapping. First, the attention that people pay to the market decreases exponentially as time goes on because people are distracted and the confirmations either show up or don't, depending on whether the trade goes through or not. And the second is, the volume validates diffusion since only replaced orders move price sustainably. Now, let's turn that first theory into an exponential decay function with a half-life measured in minutes. So, take that second theory and turn it into a volume multiplier that'll raise the effective weight when the event happens at the same time as a big volume burst. And when you combine both, you get a weighted sentiment score that shows recency and participation instead of raw counts. When you're dealing with a weighted score, don't think of it as an absolute trade trigger, treat it more like a sorting field. It's best to keep your boundaries in check so you don't get overwhelmed by someone's mood swings.

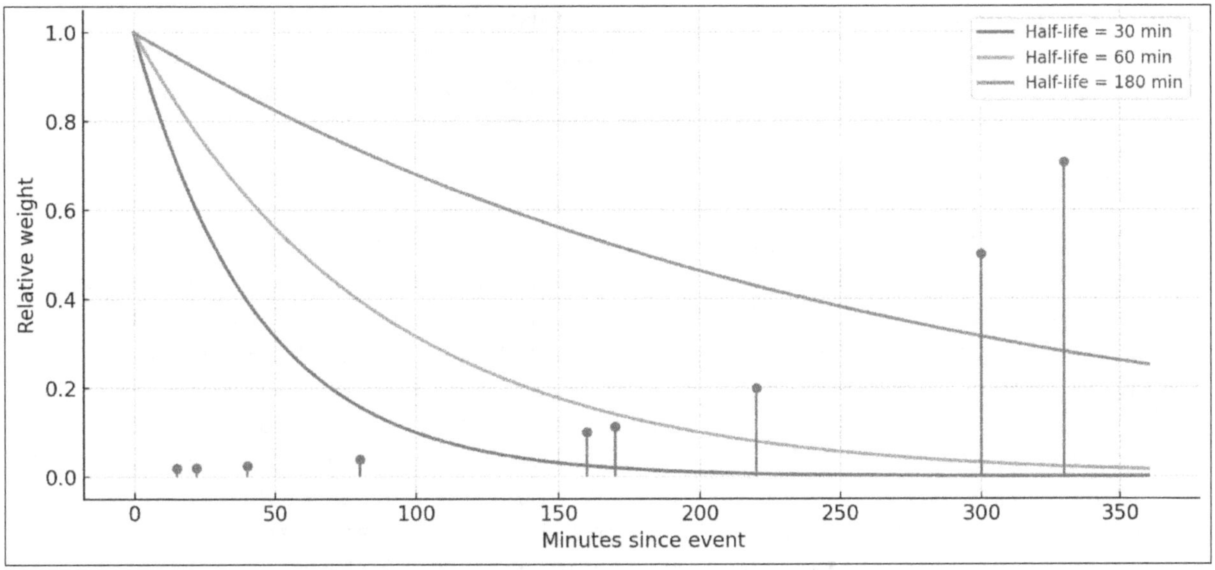

Fig 4.1 Exponential Decay Functions with Mention Timeline Overlay

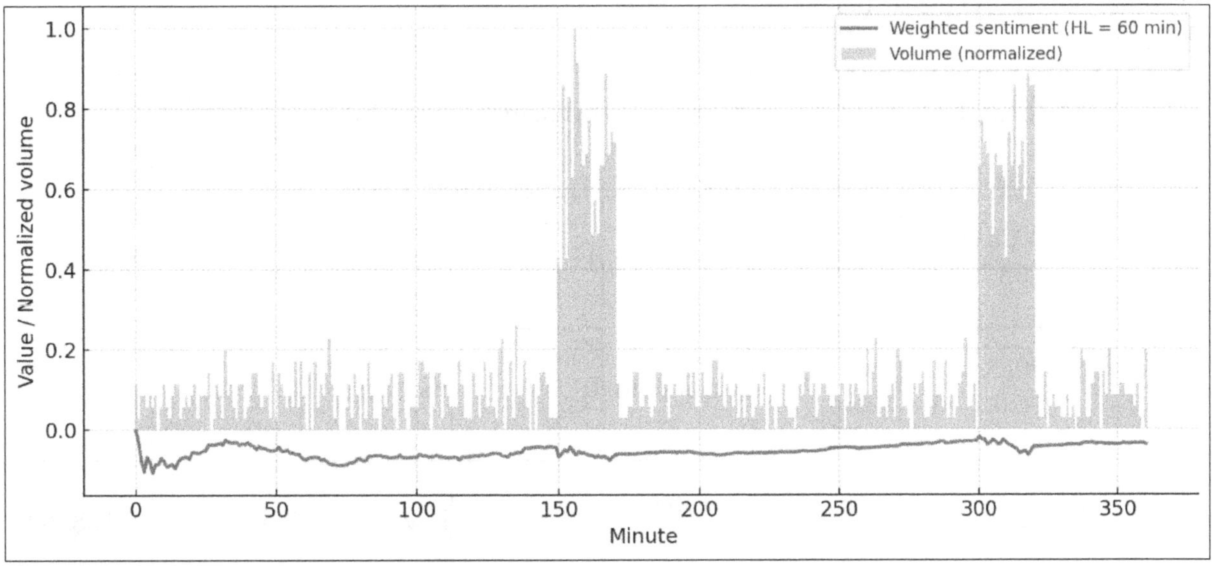

Fig 4.2 Weighted Sentiment with Volume Overlay

Decay Weighted Sentiment

To get started, just give the name of the universe and the exact time window. Then, just specify the decay parameter by choosing a half-life in minutes. The good defaults are, 30 minutes for scalps, 60 minutes for intraday reads, and 180 minutes for a broader session view. We need to define credibility weights for host types so that anonymous posts get discounted and named publishers get full weight. And when you ask for the raw counts and the decay-weighted score, don't forget to ask for a small provenance table that lists the top mentions driving the score. We only need numeric fields and timestamps for each mention. If you don't have live data or timestamps, reply with a single cell value UNKNOWN so the desk doesn't act on guessed numbers.

Following is the sample prompt:

```
For UNIVERSE over the last WINDOW minutes compute a decay
weighted social sentiment score. Apply an exponential decay
with half life HALF_LIFE minutes. Score polarity as +1 for
bullish 0 for neutral and -1 for bearish. Apply credibility
weights high 1.0 medium 0.6 low 0.3. Return a mention level
table with columns mention_time UTC local_time host domain
polarity credibility decay_weight weighted_contribution. Then
return aggregates total_mentions unique_hosts raw_balance
weighted_balance and final_weighted_score between minus one
and plus one. If live data missing reply UNKNOWN.
```

And the output table is as below:

mention_time UTC	**local_time**	**host**	**domain**	**polarity**	**credibility**	**decay_weight**	**weighted_contribution**
25/08/25 10:47	2025-08-25 16:17 IST	mobile.twitter.com	x.com	1	high	0.890899	0.890899
25/08/25 10:32	2025-08-25 16:02 IST	www.reddit.com	reddit.com	0	medium	0.749154	0
25/08/25 10:07	2025-08-25 15:37 IST	news.example.com	example.com	-1	low	0.561231	-0.168369
25/08/25 9:47	2025-08-25 15:17 IST	api.stockchat.ai	stockchat.ai	1	medium	0.445449	0.26727
25/08/25 9:22	2025-08-25 14:52 IST	www.youtube.com	youtube.com	-1	high	0.33371	-0.33371

25/08/25 9:02	2025-08-25 14:32 IST	www.finblog.net	finblog.net	1	low	0.264866	0.07946

As you can see in the above, three mentions are mentioned at 5 minutes, 30 minutes, and 120 minutes relative to the present time. For this, you will need to choose a half-life of 60 minutes. Now, to find the decay weights, just multiply 0.5 by the power of the age divided by the half-life. So for about five minutes, the weight is around 0.944. The weight is about 0.707 for 30 minutes. And for 120 minutes, the weight is 0.25. Let us say the polarities are +1, -1, and the credibility weights are 1.0, 1.0, and 0.3. Then, multiply polarity times credibility times decay weight for each mention and add up the contributions. Then, just divide the sum by the sum of absolute credibility times decay weights to get the final weighted score. The resulting number supports the recent bullish mentions and downplays the older bearish post.

Cluster Mentions and Echo Chambers

Ask the GPT to cluster mentions by domain and host family so amplification becomes visible. Request cluster keys such as domain first mention time and mention count per cluster. Keep a rule that no single domain cluster may represent more than 40 percent of unique host count before the signal is treated as broadly adopted. When concentration exceeds that share flag the item as concentrated and demand opposite side arguments before sizing. Also ask for the top three domains with credibility tags and the total unique host count. That view separates genuine broad adoption from single origin stories copied by many aggregators.

Following is the prompt to detect concentration:

```
For UNIVERSE in the last WINDOW minutes group mentions by
domain and return domain first_mention_time count unique_hosts
credibility_tag and concentration_flag true or false if domain
unique_host_share greater than 0.4. Also return
top_three_domains and total_unique_host_count. If live data
missing reply UNKNOWN.
```

The above one yields a small heatmap showing domain counts across time windows which gives instant clarity on whether a single source dominates.

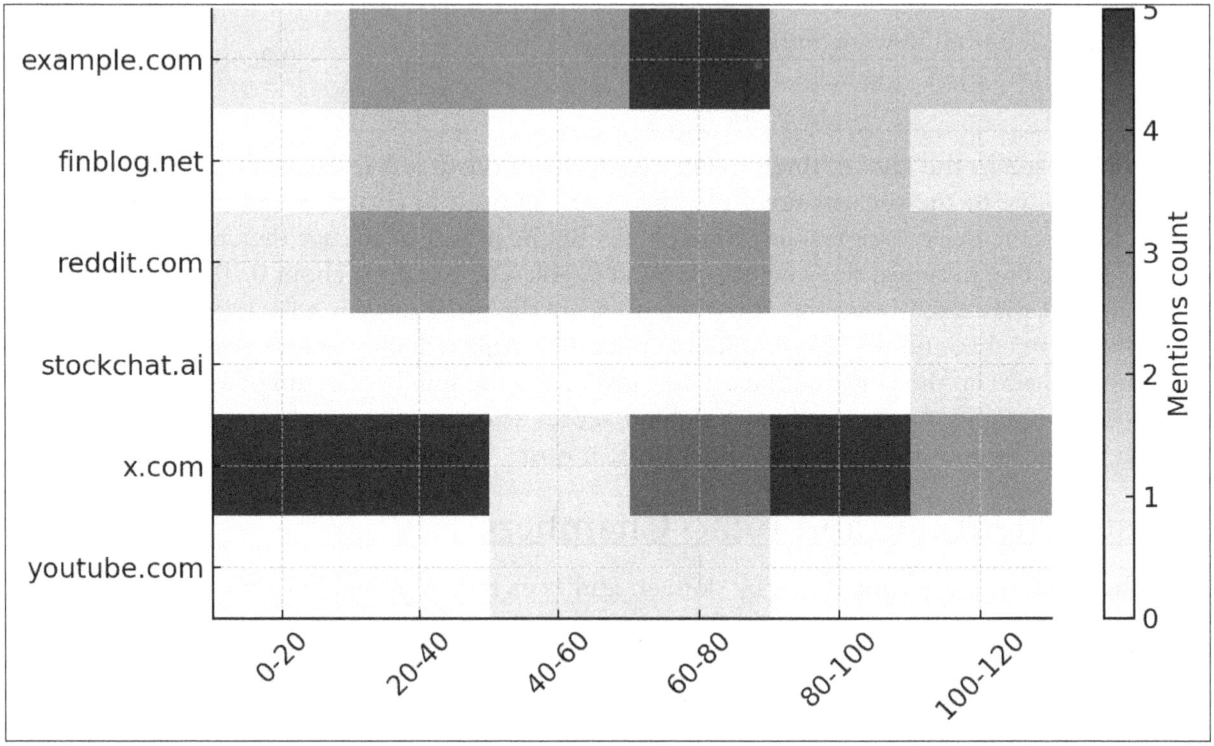

Fig 4.3 Domain Mention Counts

In addition, it will show a pie chart that shows the share of unique hosts per domain for the current window.

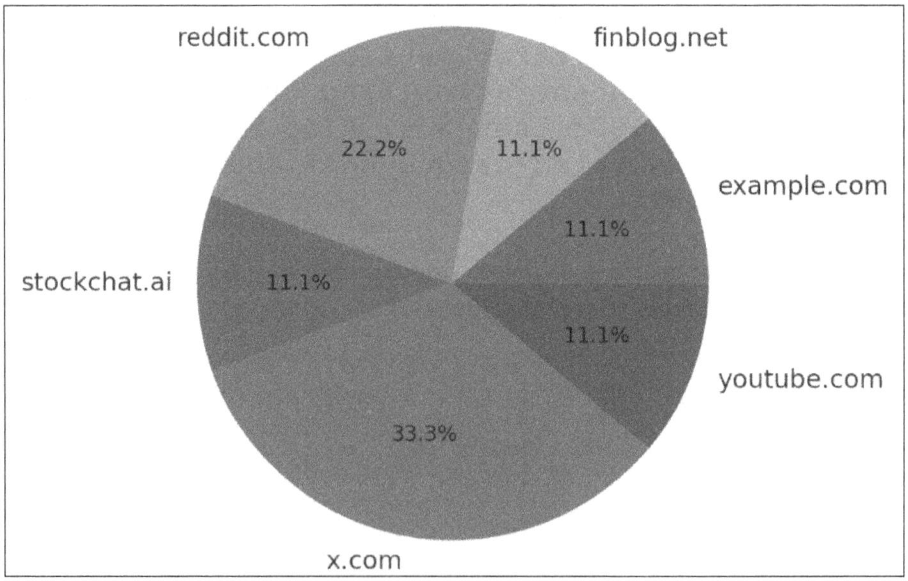

Fig 4.4 Unique Hosts Share

Balancing Opposite Side Arguments

If the weighted score is off to one side, ask the GPT to give you the top three bullish claims and the top three bearish claims. They should include the host timestamp and a one-line reason. When you're looking for a way to measure conviction, we need to ask for a numeric sentiment spread. That's basically the difference between a bullish weighted sum and a bearish weighted sum. A high spread, low concentration, and volume confirmation all point to a small mechanical plan. If the spread is wide and the concentration or volume is high, it's better to keep an eye on it instead of adding to it.

Following is a sample prompt:

```
For SYMBOL or UNIVERSE return top three bullish mentions and
top three bearish mentions in the last WINDOW minutes. For
each mention include host timestamp short_reason and
credibility_tag. Compute bullish_weighted_sum
bearish_weighted_sum and the net_sentiment_spread. Return a
numeric table and a one line tactical cue from prefer momentum
prefer fade monitor. If live data missing reply UNKNOWN.
```

This will yield a side by side table of the top bullish and top bearish mentions with timestamps and credibility tags helps form quick judgments. It will also give a small bar chart of bullish weighted contributions versus bearish weighted contributions, which then makes the net spread visually obvious.

By combining recency weighting clustering and volume validation, we can turn sentiments into actionable insights. The weighted score is just one of many inputs to consider. You should also test the approach over time to see if it works for your trading style. Things like decay curves, timelines, clustering, heatmaps, and flowcharts make it easier to learn and follow the routine.

Volume Profiling

The volume profile shows the price history as a participation map, which reveals where market participants actually agreed to trade. The areas with a lot of traded volume form nodes that act like magnets because those prices show negotiated deals between buyers and sellers and so attract interest on re tests. There are zones of low volume that look like thin tails or single prints. These zones show where there was low liquidity, so prices can speed up through them with little friction.

The value area is the price band that contains the share of session volume you picked, which is usually about seventy percent. The point of control is the single price level with the most traded volume for the session. Single prints describe isolated auction bars where there's little to no opposing interest, and those prints often mark low-friction corridors or potential stop-run zones. When the value area and point of control line up with the session structure, like the opening auction, the first hour, or a defined open range, the resulting levels gain authority because discovery and participation overlap. That interaction separates participation-based support and resistance from visual guesswork. When it comes to trading, it's best to use levels that come from participation and are based on session boundaries when setting entries, stops, and targets. If you make a profile with an even bucket size and timestamps, you can map the numeric output directly to the chart. This reduces ambiguity when you're executing live.

Core Concepts

The value area is basically the upper and lower bounds that enclose a chosen share of session volume, most commonly seventy percent. The point of control marks the single price level that had the largest traded volume for the session. When you look at single prints, they show up as isolated auction bars with little overlap, and they point to low-liquidity corridors where prices went up quickly without a lot of resistance.

The following is a short reference table clarifying the roles and what to expect from each element.

Concept	Definition	Operational signal
Value area	Price band containing the chosen share of volume for the session	Acts as a participation zone. Reentries into this band show negotiated acceptance and often offer meaningful support or resistance
Point of control	The single price with the highest traded volume	Serves as a magnet. Price drifting away from the POC often returns to test it when liquidity reappears
Single prints	Isolated price bars with thin traded volume	Indicate low liquidity passages and fast price travel. These zones can be swept by stops or act as quick rejection points

The way these anchors read changes based on session boundaries. The first part of the auction and the first regular hour are all about getting to know the lay of the land. When the value area forms inside the opening range, it suggests a negotiated balance during discovery and an increased chance of mean reversion inside that band. When the value area is way up or down from the opening range, the session shows that the market is accepting direction, and the higher side of the value area becomes a target for traders who want to build momentum. Also, point of control placement carries clear directional information. If a POC is outside the opening range, it's a signal that the price is moving away from the discovery zone. This makes it more likely that the price will continue to move in that direction until a new participation node forms. If the POC is in the opening range, it means that the discovery process ended with balanced negotiation, and the price may keep moving around the POC until a new auction forms.

If you see single prints on the high or low edges of the profile, that's a sign that price ran through thin liquidity. You can think of these areas as magnets on pullbacks when liquidity returns or as stop run corridors when a lot of resting orders build up there. I'd rather trade based on participation levels combined with session context than rely on visual guesswork. When you're working with data, it's important to always request explicit timestamps, the aggregation bucket size, and the source of profile data. This way, you can make sure that the numeric levels map precisely to the chart.

Let us take the following prompt to return clean numeric outputs that avoids guessing from pixels:

```
For SYMBOL at VENUE on SESSION_DATE return the session volume
profile over the regular session and the pre and post sessions
if available. Provide numeric fields: value_area_low
value_area_high point_of_control poc_volume poc_time
single_print_ranges as a list of price spans and their
timestamps, and session_open_range high low and open_time
close_time. Return a small table that maps these levels to
likely role support or resistance and include a concise
sentence label for context. If live data unavailable reply
UNKNOWN.
```

The expected output would be:

```
SYMBOL NASDAQ:ABC  SESSION_DATE 2025-08-25

Value_area_low 53.20

Value_area_high 55.10

Point_of_control 54.00  poc_volume 1 200 000  poc_time 09:22

Single_print_ranges [[52.90 53.00 09:05] [55.80 55.95 15:45]]

Open_range_high 54.40  Open_range_low 53.80  Open_time 09:30
Close_time 16:00

Role mapping

Value area 53.20 55.10 acts as primary participation zone
Support inside this zone is stronger than isolated intraday
lows

POC 54.00 acts as magnet when price drifts away and can be
tested on re entry
```

```
Single prints above 55.80 indicate low liquidity passage and
fast rejection likely
```

Pair Volume Profiling with Session

The first step is to figure out the session boundaries that matter for the venue. When you exchange specific opening auctions and expanded pre-market sessions, it changes how you look at things. After that, just align the value area and point of control with those boundaries. If there's a point of control within the opening range, it means that the participants negotiated there during discovery, and the price may bounce around that level. If there's a point of control outside the opening range, it suggests that the direction of acceptance is away from the initial discovery zone, and there's a higher chance of trend continuation until a new area of high participation forms. When single prints show up on the high or low edges of the profile, it's a sign that prices moved quickly through thin liquidity. In these areas, things can go either way. They might pull back when liquidity returns and become magnets, or they might have stops that cluster and fail quickly.

Following are some of the sample rules that convert levels into trades:

- When price reenters the value area from above and POC sits inside the value area, accept long setups that target the top of the value area with stops just below the POC.
- When POC lies above the open range and price breaks above the POC on high volume accept momentum entries with a target equal to measured range expansion.
- When single prints mark an isolated spike above the value area treat the spike as a low liquidity tag and prefer either a fade with tight stops or a wait for volume confirmation on re entry.

Now the best thing to do is to frame the rules as mechanical checks so the GPT can return numeric triggers and timestamps rather than narrative. This makes the output actionable without additional calculations.

Following is the sample prompt to compute actionable triggers and timestamps:

```
For SYMBOL at VENUE on SESSION_DATE return: value_area_low
value_area_high point_of_control poc_volume poc_time
single_prints list with start_price end_price start_time
end_time, session_open_range open_high open_low
open_start_time, and compute triggers: long_entry_on_reentry
price equal to top of value area plus 0.1 percent, stop_long
equals POC minus 0.25 percent, target_long equals entry plus
measured_range expansion percent. Return numeric table and one
line tactical cue. If live data unavailable reply UNKNOWN.
```

The possible output the GPT will give you is:

```
Symbol NASDAQ:ABC Time 10:05 Last_price 54.20

Value_area 53.20 55.10 POC 54.00 poc_time 09:22

Trigger long_entry_on_reentry 55.15 stop_long 53.65
target_long 56.80

Tactical cue prefer momentum entry on confirmed reentry
volume_ratio 1.8
```

Now here, if you need the source of the profile data or the aggregation bucket size (like 1 minute or 5 minutes), just ask the GPT. If the profile buckets don't match the chart template, just reject the output and ask for them to be aggregated again.

Turning Raw Feeds to Tradable Edges

Feeds to Edges Benefits

While markets do respond to information, not all information leads to tradable opportunities. The research on market microstructure shows how price changes are influenced by the flow and liquidity of the market. The academic work that links order flow to price impact shows that big trades with liquidity often lead to follow through, while chatter without capital often doesn't pan out. There's a lot of info out there on auction market theory, and a lot of it says that participation nodes are reliable anchors and that single prints are thin liquidity passages. When you combine those perspectives, you can turn raw feeds into a usable signal set by forcing verification and by measuring participation. This approach uses the same kind of academic rigor and practicality of desk heuristics, so you end up with a checklist that can be used in every session.

Our raw feeds include headlines, social mentions, options sweeps, block trades, and volume bursts. There's a tradable edge when a feed item passes three tests at once: it has a directional bias, it aligns to participation based levels, and it survives an invalidation test. With directional bias, you can see who's interested in the position. Participation-based levels show where the two sides matched. The invalidation test shows where the thesis falls short and how much risk is involved. Just treat the conversion as mechanical. A single sentence cue like "prefer momentum" or "prefer fade" just won't cut it unless it's attached to specific numeric levels, catalysts, and an explicit invalidation level. If you make a checklist with bias levels, catalysts, and invalidation clauses, you will have a compact decision card that's easy to read under stress.

Checklist Components

The checklist has four sections:

1. The first field is biased. There are short tags like "bullish," "bearish," or "neutral," and they go with a numeric score from -2 to +2. The GPT gives both direction and intensity.

2. The second field is levels. We need to provide exact numeric levels for entry support, resistance, and invalidation with timestamps and a source label.
3. The third field is catalysts. For each catalyst, include the primary and secondary catalysts, along with the host tags and a short note explaining why the catalyst is important to the price.
4. The fourth field is about invalidating something. We need to give a precise price that cancels the idea and a stop sizing suggestion expressed as a percentage of equity or percentage of the average true range so sizing rules remain reproducible.

The checklist also has small meta fields, like time horizon, target windows, and a quick note on typical liquidity for the ticker so the plan fits the desk style.

Tradable Edge Checklist Template

This single page checklist converts raw market feeds into a compact actionable plan. It forces verification, captures participation driven levels, sets invalidation and specifies sizing. The template fits a single screen and can be pasted into a trade journal or saved as a reusable prompt template.

Top Level Fields

Field	**What to put here**	**Why it matters?**
Symbol	Exchange prefixed ticker for example NASDAQ:NVDA	Avoids wrong instrument lookup
Interval	Chart candle size for analysis for example 5m or 1m	Aligns numbers to chart candles
Date time	ISO timestamp for the snapshot in UTC for example 2025-08-25T09:28Z	Anchors all levels to an exact candle
Bias tag	One of bullish bearish neutral	Directional intent for the idea
Conviction	Integer scale minus two minus one zero one two	Expresses strength of the bias

Levels Block

Here, you enter each level with numeric value timestamp UTC and source label. And then , keep the block short so it fits one screen.

Level	Price	Timestamp UTC	Source
Entry			
Support			
Resistance			
Invalidation			

The entry could be a conditional trigger or a price to watch for immediate execution. You have to be clear about invalidation. For example, a price that cancels the thesis and prompts exit. For the source, you will want to use either TradingView or an exchange feed for price levels, and for catalysts, a named publisher.

Catalysts Block

This lists the primary, and then the secondary catalysts. And, each entry requires a one line reason timestamp and a source link or host label.

Role	Timestamp UTC	Source host or link	Short reason (<12 words)
Primary catalyst			
Secondary catalyst			

Risk and Sizing Block

Field	Value example	Notes

Suggested size	1 percent equity	Or ATR multiple such as 0.5 ATR
Stop method	Fixed price or ATR based	Example stop equals entry minus 0.7 percent
Time horizon	Intraday or multi session	Guides target setting

Actionable Summary Line

This is just a short line that the desk can read without parsing the full checklist. And it is limited to ten words or less.

For example, it could be something like:

```
Action prefer momentum entry 416 stop 412 target 423 size 1
pct
```

Below is the sample template for NVDA stock:

```
CHECKLIST
Symbol NASDAQ:NVDA
Interval 5m
Snapshot 2025-08-25T09:28Z
Bias bullish Conviction 1
Levels
Entry 416.00 2025-08-25T09:28Z TradingView
Support 412.00 2025-08-25T09:28Z POC
Resistance 423.00 2025-08-25T09:28Z Recent high
Invalidation 411.00 2025-08-25T09:28Z Stop level
Catalysts
Primary 2025-08-25T09:25Z Bloomberg revenue surprise
Secondary 2025-08-25T09:20Z BrokerX options sweep
Risk Sizing
Suggested size 1 percent equity
Stop method fixed price 0.7 percent below entry
```

```
Time horizon intraday
Action line prefer momentum entry 416 stop 412 target 423
size 1 pct
```

Putting together a tidy checklist turns feeds into clear plans that line up directly with the chart and orders. You really need to save the template and keep practicing this short task a lot so the workflow becomes second nature. The more the iterations you run, it will reduce false positives and produce a reliable set of mechanical trades that transform raw feeds into genuine tradable edges.

Summary

Basically, we looked at how sentiment and sudden volume interacted to produce intraday price moves and how volume spikes often validated narrative. We modeled social mood with exponential decay, so older mentions carried less weight. It's like credibility weighting favored named publishers over anonymous posts, and clustering showed us echo chambers that needed opposite side arguments for balance. We really went into the nitty-gritty of volume profile concepts, talking about value area, point of control, and single prints as anchors, not just for show, but for practical purposes. We've got all the info you need to calculate the value area and POC, including timestamps, bucket sizes, and provenance.

We also came up with a short list of things to remember to convert feed signals into bias levels, catalysts, numeric entry and invalidation rules, and sizing and time horizon. They recommended using archival and weekly scoring routines to tune half-life thresholds, credibility tags, and trigger rules. A feedback loop linked checklist outcomes to price paths, so historical follow-through rates guided future parameter adjustments. It's like they were programmed to work like a well-oiled machine, cutting down on decision-making time and noise.

Chapter 6: Single-Ticker Intraday Live Prompting

Pre-Market Prep

So far, we've learned a lot about how to use AI for day-to-day trading and to make the most of sentiments, news, stock volume, technical indicators, past performance of the stock, and the ability of TradingView to show the stock's real-time price movements. We've found that keeping things clean and organized leads to consistent results. We had to use persona declarations and fixed output shapes to make sure the numeric fields, timestamps, and source labels were in place so the responses could be mapped directly to charts. Decay weighted sentiment turned noisy mentions into measurable scores. We used volume profile techniques to come up with participation-based levels, like value area and point of control, which we used as operational anchors. The abnormal activity triage gave us z scores, range ratios, and persistence counts, so we could focus on the unusual events. Before each event, the calendar checks the attached pre-event buffers and risk labels so exposure can be adjusted. The checklist turned raw feeds into bias levels, catalysts, numeric entries, and explicit invalidation. So, all these elements come together to let you do a quick analysis in the morning. The result is a single decision card for one symbol, which includes the overnight context, headlines, event risk, a primary thesis, and a backup plan.

Routine Ritual before Market Begins

As a general rule, it's best to start the ritual at least 30 minutes before the trading window opens. That way, you will have enough time to settle the feeds and check your charting platform for visual confirmation. We will keep the session persona and the output shape the same so every morning gives you the same cells in the same order. If you keep the shape fixed, you can shorten the scan step and make the checklist paste friendly for a trade note or for quick manual order entry. Also, make sure to archive every snapshot with the symbol timestamp, channel, and the raw mentions. That way, you will have a replayable record for scoring later. Over time, that archive becomes the go-to tool for calibrating half-life credibility weights and volume thresholds for promotion into the active rotation.

In a nutshell, a single ritual tied together four tasks into one easy-to-follow flow. First, get the overnight price context and figure out the gap metrics so the opening's got a clear anchor. Second, collect the top headlines across the overnight window and score each by credibility and by concentration so you can see the narrative risk. Third, check the economic calendar and any exchange notices that affect execution rules. Fourth, make a decision card that's short and sweet, with a main idea and a backup plan with clear numbers and a suggested size.

Following is a quick example to show what we're aiming for and make it clear what the outcome should be:

```
Persona Technical strategist with an absolute no guess policy.
```

```
Objective Produce a pre market snapshot for NASDAQ:TSLA at
TradingView. Return a compact table with these fields:
snapshot_time_utc last_price local_time overnight_high
overnight_low overnight_range percent_gap gap_direction
proximity_to_overnight_high proximity_to_overnight_low
top_three_headlines with timestamp host short_catalyst
credibility_tag concentration_flag events_in_open_window with
pre_buffer_minutes and impact_label value_area_low
value_area_high point_of_control poc_time single_prints list
suggested_primary_thesis one line suggested_backup_path one
line suggested_size_percent invalidation_price. Return numeric
fields only. If live data missing reply UNKNOWN.
```

This will give us a solid output, basically a table with all the necessary info from the GPT. This'll help us get a handle on the stock that's up for grabs today. Once you get this, we will run these verification steps:

- Check the overnight high, overnight low, percent_gap, and last_price against your chart. If any field says "UNKNOWN," go ahead and run the targeted verification prompt for that field.
- If percent_gap is good to go, go ahead and reduce suggested_size and tighten invalidation.
- If point_of_control is outside the overnight band, go ahead and mark the session as a directional acceptance event.
- If overnight_range is really thin, it's better to wait for participation instead of using ladder-sized entries.

Compute Gap Context and Flags

We will be anchoring the prior session close and extended hours' extremes according to the venue definition. You can calculate percent_gap by taking the difference between the first_regular_open and prior_close, and then dividing that by the prior_close multiplied by 100. We can find the overnight range by taking the extended high and subtracting the extended low. Go with the averages from the last five sessions as a starting point. If the overnight range is less than half of that baseline, mark it as thin. A good rule of thumb is to choose a gap significance threshold of about 1.5%, but you can adjust that based on historical data. If thresholds are breached, give the desk both the raw numbers and flag values so they can get a handle on the situation at once.

Following is the sample numeric snapshot that matched the checklist shape:

```
Snapshot 2025-08-26T09:00Z Last_price 265.40 Local_time 05:30
ET Overnight_high 274.20 Overnight_low 258.00 Overnight_range
16.20 Percent_gap 3.20 Gap_direction up Proximity_to_high 3.18
percent Proximity_to_low 2.83 percent Gap_flag SIGNIFICANT
Range_flag NORMAL
```

Top Headlines and Fast Verification

For the overnight window, we need the top three headlines with the host's timestamp, a one-line catalyst tag, and a credibility label. If you're making claims that could change exposure, make sure you have direct links. We should only run the short verification prompt for headlines that would alter size or the plan. When the headline says "CONFIRMED" and the volume goes up, put the candidate on the active watchlist with a smaller initial size. If the headline comes back as UNKNOWN, move the ticker to the monitor bucket and make sure it's verified or cleared for participation before sizing it.

Following is the verification prompt for headline checks:

```
Persona Technical strategist with an absolute no guess policy.

Objective For the headline "SHORT HEADLINE" search the last 90
minutes and return up to two independent confirmations with
host timestamp and direct link to the primary source. Return
verification status CONFIRMED or UNKNOWN. If live data
unavailable reply UNKNOWN.
```

Event Risk and Pre-Event Buffers

Also, when you're requesting calendar items, try to pick ones that fall within the pre-market buffer or during the opening hour. And don't forget to tag each item with the region, asset class, and impact label. For high-impact events, go ahead and attach a pre-buffer in minutes and a cash-advice flag. If Cash Advise comes back as TRUE, hold off on adding size before the event. If something happens in the market that affects more than one asset, like a big economic report, it'll be smaller across the board.

Following is the sample event block:

```
Event US CPI 13 30 UTC Local 09 30 ET Impact HIGH Pre buffer
30 Cash advised TRUE Affected asset classes equities bonds FX
```

Primary Thesis and Backup Path Construction

The main idea should be written as one clear sentence that explains the direction, trigger levels, and exact conditions for execution. So, just write the backup path as one sentence. In that sentence, describe the alternative scenario and the invalidation that cancels the thesis. Just make sure to attach numeric levels and timestamps to both plans so the open doesn't require ad hoc thinking.

Following is the sample filled plan:

```
Primary thesis Prefer momentum on break above 118.25 Entry
118.35 Stop 117.80 Target 121.00 Size 0.5 percent equity

Backup path Prefer fade on rejection above 118 Entry 117.90
Stop 118.50 Target 116.20 Size 0.3 percent equity
```

Final Checks and Archive Ritual

And here, double-check that every numeric cell has a source label and a timestamp. If there are any unknown fields, run the targeted verification prompt. And then save the filled checklist with the session ID and timestamp to the archive. When you open the chart, check the overnight extremes, value area, and point of control. The first candles form run the minute level execution prompt that maps checklist levels to active orders. Also, make sure you archive the results and calculate the follow-through metrics at five minutes, 30 minutes, and four hours. This will help refine the thresholds and half-life parameters on a weekly basis.

You may simply ask for a visual infographic for it, like a decay curve figure for the half life chosen for sentiment, a compact snapshot image showing overnight extremes value area and point of control side by side with the filled checklist, a small table that shows headline confirmations and their timestamps, or a flowchart that maps the ritual from snapshot to verification to archive will make the routine easy to adopt.

It's a piece of cake for the pros to run the whole thing in under three minutes when the feeds are stable. If verification is needed, plan for about ten minutes. You should also archive every run and let weekly scoring guide small parameter changes so the approach becomes faster and more accurate over time.

Opening Range and First Decision

We also learned how a persona and objective routine produced compact numeric tables with timestamps and source labels. We used a decay weighted sentiment routine to convert noisy mentions into measurable scores. The abnormal activity triage showed participation-driven moves with Z scores and persistence counts. The volume profile levels gave us participation-based anchors, and the tradable edge checklist turned raw feeds into a single decision card. These inputs came in right at the start, so the first step was to focus on one thing: making a one-page plan that included the opening range high and low, the early volume read, and momentum alignment. This would make sure decisions were based on rules and not on impulse. One rule set prevented opening fear of missing out by enforcing verification and by demanding numeric confirmation before any size was added.

Fifteen Minutes and Early Volume

To be honest, we used the first fifteen minutes of the regular session for the opening range. The 15-minute interval hit a nice balance between speed and noise, giving traders a clear reference point to trade around. Also, you will need to figure out the opening range high and low and add timestamps for the high and low candles. After that, figure out the opening range width and compare it to a rolling baseline, like the last ten opening range widths, to get a range ratio. When the range ratio is more than two, it's a sign of a wide opening range, which usually means there's going to be some early volatility.

And when you're figuring out the opening range, it's a good idea to pair it with an early volume read. For each contract or share traded, we measure the total for the opening range and compare that to the average from the same fifteen-minute window across the prior five sessions. If the data allows, express the result as a ratio and calculate a z score. When the volume ratio was above 1.5 and the z score was above 2, it was a pretty solid sign that the volume was confirmed. That confirmation made it more likely that if the opening range broke, it would hold and not quickly fade.

Let us try out the TSLA example. At first, we will run the first prompt to return opening range levels and timestamps plus volume comparison and a short momentum snapshot:

```
Persona Technical strategist with an absolute no guess policy.

Objective For NASDAQ:TSLA on TradingView compute the opening
range using the first 15 minutes of regular session. Return:
OR_high OR_high_time OR_low OR_low_time OR_width
OR_range_ratio volume_within_OR avg_volume_baseline
volume_ratio volume_zscore early_momentum MA9 MA21 RSI14 VWAP
and a one line cue that summarizes whether conditions favored
participating in a break or waiting. Return numeric fields
only. If live data missing reply UNKNOWN.
```

This will yield us with an opening range output and this we can then use it for our quick chart checks:

```
OR_high 275.40 OR_high_time 09:46:00 OR_low 271.80 OR_low_time
09:32:00 OR_width 3.60 OR_range_ratio 1.85

Volume_within_OR 2 100 000 Avg_volume_baseline 1 200 000
Volume_ratio 1.75 Volume_zscore 2.4

MA9 273.50 MA21 272.10 RSI14 61 VWAP 273.85
```

```
One line cue prefer participate on break when volume ratio >=
1.5 and RSI > 55 otherwise wait
```

Now the next question that will immediately pop in is, how to read the numbers very quickly? So here, a range ratio near two with volume ratio above 1.5 is suggesting a genuine opening discovery rather than a noise driven spike. The moving average tilt and the RSI gave quick momentum alignment confirming direction. The one-line cue translated the numeric read into a rule to follow during the first hour.

Now the next question that arises is whether to act or wait? So here too, I have identified three conditions that have to be true simultaneously before we can add size. The conditions are:

1. Price closed beyond the opening range on the chosen execution interval for example a close above OR_high on a one-minute bar.
2. Volume confirmation on the break with volume ratio > 1.5 and volume z score > 2 in the break bar or the immediate following bar.
3. Momentum alignment with MA9 above MA21 and RSI above 55 for bullish plays or the reverse for bearish plays.

Now, if all three conditions met, the plan allowed a small initial size such as 0.5 percent of equity with a tight invalidation set to either a percent rule or the opposite opening range edge. If any condition failed, the plan required waiting for re-entry conditions such as a re-test of the opening range with confirmed participation or a clear trend of higher highs or lower lows over the next N bars.

Fallback Rules for FOMO

Once the price breaks free from the opening range but doesn't pass the participation test, it's time to follow a few simple rules to keep things under control. To start, set the immediate action size to zero and move the idea to the watchlist for the next confirmation loop. And second, any later entry should show a re-test with volume confirmation and momentum alignment. The third thing to do is to set a time window for the watchlist rule. We're talking about ten to twenty-five minutes after the opening. After that, the idea is either promoted or archived. That time window stopped constant monitoring and made waiting into a decision step.

Following is a sample prompt that provide minute level checks using shorter bars to catch fast moves:

```
Persona Technical strategist with an absolute no guess policy.
```

```
Objective For NASDAQ:TSLA on TradingView return minute level
checks for the first three minutes after a close beyond
OR_high. If price closes above OR_high on a one minute bar
compute entry limit as next tick price round two decimals
compute stop as OR_low minus 0.4 percent compute target as
entry plus measured range expansion percent and compute
expected slippage as spread plus one tick. Return
volume_on_break volume_ratio_on_break momentum MA9 MA21 RSI14
and suggested_entry stop and target. If data missing reply
UNKNOWN.
```

This above prompt will give a minute level output and execution cue as below:

```
Break_bar_time 09:48:00 Volume_on_break 420 000
Volume_ratio_on_break 2.1 Momentum MA9 275.90 MA21 273.60
RSI14 64

Suggested_entry 276.05 Stop 272.91 Target 281.40
Expected_slippage 0.08

Action place limit entry 276.05 stop 272.91 target 281.40 size
0.5 percent equity
```

Here, the minute level check prevented reliance on a single higher timeframe candle that lacked flow and reminded the trader to account for spread via the expected slippage cell.

Trade Plan with Sizing and Exits

All we do is take a snapshot and turn it into a contract. When you've got a short trade plan, it says how much you want to enter, the target size, and the rules for making adjustments. That way, the desk acts from the plan instead of from impulse. The risk units that are fixed make things consistent across trades, so you can always predict how much exposure there will be. Below, we will go over how to set an entry price and a stop based on participation levels, how to figure out position size from a fixed risk unit, and how to add explicit exit rules linked to levels and time.

Defining Plan Elements

We've got a trade plan that fits on a single page and requires five fields. The first field is "entry," where you describe a specific trigger, like a limit on a breakout, a market order on confirmed close, or a conditional order on a retest. The second field is the "stop" field. Here, you put in a price that cancels out the thesis. This price should reflect the liquidity context instead of an arbitrary percentage. The third field is called "target" where you put in a number or a series of profit levels and connect them to measured moves or participation-based levels. The fourth field is "size" which is expressed as a function of a fixed risk unit that the desk keeps constant across trades. The last field is "timing" where we tie the plan to a time window that defines when the plan expires and when a fresh assessment becomes required. For each field, there's a timestamp and a source label so that the plan can be audited.

Fixed Risk Unit Sizing

A fixed risk unit makes managing capital easier. A risk unit is basically a percentage of equity. For an account worth $100,000, a risk unit at 0.5% is equal to $500 per trade. The size of your position is equal to the risk unit divided by the risk per share. That's the absolute difference between your entry and your stop.

Once you get the hang of it, you can just keep going with the math. Let us say you bought at 276.05 and sold at 272.91. The share risk is 3.14 dollars. To figure this out, we took 276.05 and subtracted 272.91. If you take a 500-dollar risk unit and divide it by 3.14, you get about 159.23 shares. And just a heads-up, you will want to round down to avoid fractional shares, so make sure your position size is 159 shares. The position dollar value is 159 times 276.05, which equals 43,891.95 dollars. The percentage of equity allocated is equal to the position dollar value divided by the equity, which equals 43.89%. The fixed risk unit sizing keeps the maximum dollar loss the same, but lets the position exposure float with a stop width. This means the risk per trade stays the same no matter how volatile things are.

Following is the quick reference table for the sample math:

Item	Value
Risk unit	0.5 percent
Equity	100,000
Risk unit dollars	500
Entry	276.05
Stop	272.91
Per share risk	3.14

Shares floor	159
Position value	43,891.95
Percent of equity	43.89 percent

Setting Relative Stops

A stop is basically like the plan's cancel button. When you're working on these, make sure to place stops at logical levels, like below the point of control, below a value area edge, or below a clearly tested support level. When trading single prints or thin liquidity bands, it's better to use tighter stops because they're more likely to be accepted, even if there's a small chance of a sweep. When trades reference broad participation nodes, it's better to use wider stops that allow noise inside the node.

When you're picking your entry method, make sure to always tie the stop width. If you're looking to put a limit entry above a breakout, the stop might be at the opposite opening range edge. If you're doing a re-test, the stop might be a little bit higher than the re-test low or the session micro low. We can express stop rules in numeric terms so the GPT can easily calculate sizes. For example, stop equals entry minus 0.4 percent or stop equals POC minus 0.3 percent.

Target Rules and Profit Schedules

Every target needs a reason. When it comes to measured move targets, you can go with the opening range width or a profile derived measured move. When the POC and the value area align above the breakout, it's fair to set a larger target. And for the usual stuff, just plan for some profit taking at one or two points, and link it to clear triggers. A simple split works well. You can take one-third at the first target and let the rest run with a trailing stop set below a moving average or to a fraction of ATR. So, for instance, take one-third at the start, plus OR_width, and move the stop to breakeven on the rest. Then, you can adjust the stop by 0.5 ATR or by a fixed percent per time unit. The rules for mechanical follow-ups stop ad hoc exits that can weaken the edge.

Time-based, Forced Exits and Size Scaling Rules

Risk is defined by time. If the plan says to look at intraday, then make a forced exit at the end of the session you're planning to watch or at a set number of minutes after you start. For example, set a forced exit for the remaining size at four hours after entry or at the close of the regular session, whichever comes first. When you're dealing with news events that are on the schedule, it's a good idea to put in a bit of a buffer before the print and exit positions. If a position isn't filled by the time the intended window is over, go back and recalculate the original thesis before adding size or extending stops.

There are rules about adding to winners and preventing emotional averaging into losers. For now, just use one initial size that matches the fixed risk unit. You can add smaller increments when you see that the first step is working, like half the initial risk unit per add. Also, the total scaling is set to a multiple of the risk unit, like no more than two times the initial risk unit. You should make each add conditional on fresh volume confirmation and momentum alignment. Each add recalculates the stop so the total risk stays within the planned dollar risk. For example, the initial risk unit is $500. You can add one at 250 bucks, but only if the volume ratio and momentum conditions meet the checklist thresholds. If the desk moves the stop outward to protect against slippage while keeping overall risk the same, update the position average price and recompute the stop.

Sample Prompt of Complete Plan Block

If you want strict numeric outputs, just paste the prompt after the persona line. The GPT returns a single block that can be pasted into a trade journal.

```
Persona Technical strategist with an absolute no guess policy.

Objective For NASDAQ:TSLA on TradingView return a trade plan
block for entry 276.05 stop 272.91 and risk unit percent 0.5
percent with equity 100000. Return fields: entry stop
per_share_risk risk_unit_dollars shares position_value
percent_of_equity suggested_partial_levels first_target
second_target trailing_stop_rule time_horizon add_rule
max_total_risk and a one line action cue. Return numeric
values only. If data missing reply UNKNOWN.
```

The following is the expected and the desired trade plan block from GPT:

```
Entry 276.05 Stop 272.91 Per_share_risk 3.14 Risk_unit 500
Shares 159 Position_value 43891.95 Percent_of_equity 43.89

Partial_levels 1 1 1 at 279.65 take one third at 284.00 take
remainder

Trailing_stop_rule move stop to entry on first fill then trail
at 0.5 ATR

Time_horizon intraday forced exit at close Add_rule allow one
add at 0.5 risk unit when volume_ratio>1.5 and RSI>60
Max_total_risk 1.5 percent equity

Action place limit entry 276.05 stop 272.91 size 159
```

When you've got a strict plan with fixed risk unit sizing, you don't have to guess about exposure. That makes it so you can turn an idea into a repeatable trade. The GPT gives you the numbers with exact stops, so you don't have to do the math yourself and can get things done faster. Also, make sure you archive the plan outcomes and calculate the basic follow-through metrics so you can refine your risk units, stop placement, and add rules. Eventually, the archive will adjust its size and stop cleaning, so the desk will improve its edge.

Midday Maintenance

We started with a plan that was ready to go, and we brought some initial positions into the session with small size and clear invalidations. The whole point of midday maintenance is to answer three simple operational questions at fixed checkpoints:

- Is the thesis still valid?
- Is the volume still confirming the move?
- Have any new catalysts appeared that change the risk?

When you're working on the maintenance loop, just think of it as a short ritual that a trader runs at a set time. For example, thirty minutes after the market opens and again at the mid-session mark. The ritual puts a lot of checks on a single page, so the desk can decide to tighten exposure, reduce size, or stand down. If you have a reliable midday routine, you can protect your capital by turning uncertainty into clear action steps instead of making random adjustments based on your gut.

Vitality for Live Desks

The live trading session can change quickly. If the early momentum becomes the market price, then it'll stay that way as long as the participants keep adding size. But if there's not enough liquidity, then it'll fall apart. And midday maintenance helps keep you from going from a tentative idea to a huge regret. It's best to run the maintenance routine when the market has calmed down after the opening noise and before longer-term session rotations create new regime signals. The routine should give you a short numeric table and a one-line tactical cue that reads like an order. The table is anchored to the chart with timestamps and source labels so the numbers can be verified in seconds. When we make this a regular thing, the desk learns faster because each archived maintenance record links the pre-event plan to the real-time path and the decision that was made. So, weekly scoring shows which prompts and thresholds actually predicted follow-through.

Sample Midday Routine

A compact checklist fits on one screen. The first field is about whether the thesis is valid. You will need to ask for a one-line restatement of the original thesis and a numeric confirmation that key levels remain intact. The second field is volume confirmation. For this, we need to ask for the volume ratio and for a simple persistence count that shows whether heavy flows repeat over successive bars. The third field is called "Catalyst Update." In that field, we ask for new headlines or filings with timestamps and a credibility tag. The fourth field is about the price structure. It asks if the price made higher highs or lower lows compared to the opening range, and if the POC shifted. The fifth field is Action, which gives you one of three options: tighten, size, reduce, watch, or follow through. We've got to make sure the GPT only returns numeric cells and a one-line action cue. This way, the structure keeps human decisions short and auditable.

Following is the prompt:

```
Persona Technical strategist with an absolute no guess policy.

Objective For NASDAQ:TSLA on TradingView revalidate the
opening thesis. Return fields: thesis_statement, last_price
with timestamp, key_levels list with level type value and
timestamp, price_structure summary higher_highs lower_lows or
neutral, invalidation_status true or false and
invalidation_price. Return numeric fields and short phrases
only. If live data missing reply UNKNOWN.

Persona Technical strategist with an absolute no guess policy.

Objective For NASDAQ:TSLA compute volume confirmation for the
last 60 minutes. Return fields: volume_ratio
relative_to_5session_15min_baseline zscore persistence_count
bars_with_abnormal_volume and a boolean volume_confirm that is
true when volume_ratio >= 1.5 and zscore >= 2 and
persistence_count >= 2. Return numeric fields only. If live
data missing reply UNKNOWN.

Persona Technical strategist with an absolute no guess policy.

Objective For NASDAQ:TSLA scan the last 90 minutes for new
catalysts. Return up to three items with fields: timestamp UTC
host short_catalyst credibility_tag and verification_status
CONFIRMED DISPUTED or UNKNOWN. If no new catalyst return NONE.
If live data missing reply UNKNOWN.
```

The above prompts will output the following, and we will nowlook into how to read them quickly:

```
Thesis_statement momentum on break above OR_high 275.40 with
invalidation at OR_low 271.80

Last_price 09:58 274.20
```

```
Key_levels OR_high 275.40 09:46 OR_low 271.80 09:32 POC 273.95
09:22

Price_structure neutral

Invalidation_status false invalidation_price 271.80

Volume_ratio 1.82 zscore 2.1 persistence_count 3
bars_with_abnormal_volume 3 volume_confirm true

09:40 Bloomberg TSLA files minor software patch press release
credibility high verification CONFIRMED

09:18 Twitter unknown social post credibility low verification
UNKNOWN
```

When you see a high volume confirmation and a confirmed catalyst that's in line with the direction, it's a sign that you can hold and think about making a small addition when the next participation trigger comes up. If the volume confirmation is wrong or we don't know what the catalyst is, then we will have to go with the plan to reduce the size and wait and see what happens. When invalidation becomes true, go ahead and close the position as planned and archive the moment for scoring.

Decision Rules to Tighten Stand Down

Think of ways to turn the checklist into something that can be done. We will start with the first gate risks:

- If "invalidation_status" is set to "true," then you should exit right away to stop.

The second gate is open to participation:

- If "volume_confirm" is set to true and "price_structure" shows "higher_highs" for a bullish thesis, then keep the initial size and consider adding only if the next break bar volume ratio exceeds 2.0.

The third gate catalyst alignment:

- If a new confirmed catalyst goes against the thesis, like a negative regulatory update for a bullish thesis, then just reduce the size to zero and move the ticker to a monitor list until there's a retest with confirmed participation.

We're still a bit uncertain about the fourth gate.

- If "volume_confirm" is set to "false" and the catalysts are unknown, then just cut the size in half and tighten the stops to a narrower invalidation, like the opposite opening range edge or a fixed percent from the entry point, whichever is tighter.

And the fifth one is a gate time-based closure.

- If the position isn't filled by midday, set a forced exit at a modest profit or at a tight stop to release capital into better opportunities.

Summary

At the end of this chapter, we had a clear set of operational habits that turned intraday ideas into repeatable trades. Now we know how to make a one-page plan with timestamps, participation metrics, and minute-level execution checks. We practiced converting range and volume signals into numeric entry, stop, and target rules, as well as a fixed risk unit that kept dollar loss steady across volatility regimes.

We did a midday maintenance ritual to revalidate the thesis volume confirmation and catalyst updates so decisions were based on rules instead of feelings. We learned a thing or two about hygiene:

- Don't use live data when it's missing.
- Label uncertain claims.
- Keep track of provenance with timestamps.

All this helps to keep trust high. Ultimately, the chapter left us with a short ritual and replayable archive that made each session a training loop for better prompts and cleaner execution.

Thank You

www.ingramcontent.com/pod-product-compliance
Lightning Source LLC
Chambersburg PA
CBHW061222240926
51846CB00006B/1314

* 9 7 8 9 3 4 9 1 7 4 7 8 8 *